In a Green Shade

RICHARD MABEY

In a Green Shade

Essays on Landscape 1970–1983

Hutchinson
London Melbourne Sydney Auckland Johannesburg

Hutchinson & Co. (Publishers) Ltd

An imprint of the Hutchinson Publishing Group

17–21 Conway Street, London W1P 6JD

Hutchinson Group (Australia) Pty Ltd
30–32 Cremorne Street, Richmond South, Victoria 3121
PO Box 151, Broadway, New South Wales 2007

Hutchinson Group (NZ) Ltd
32–34 View Road, PO Box 40-086, Glenfield, Auckland 10

Hutchinson Group (SA) Pty Ltd
PO Box 337, Bergvlei 2012, South Africa

First published 1983
© Richard Mabey 1983

Set in Linotron Palatino by
Rowland Phototypesetting Ltd, Bury St Edmunds, Suffolk

Printed and bound in Great Britain by The Anchor Press Ltd
and bound by Wm Brendon & Son Ltd
both of Tiptree, Essex

British Library Cataloguing in Publication Data
Mabey, Richard
    In a green shade.
    1. Country life—Great Britain.   2. Natural
    history—Great Britain
    I. Title
    941.085′8′0924   S522.G7

ISBN 0 09 154320 7

What wond'rous Life is this I lead!
Ripe Apples drop about my head;
The Luscious Clusters of the Vine
Upon my Mouth do crush their Wine;
The Nectaren, and curious Peach,
Into my hands themselves do reach;
Stumbling on Melons, as I pass,
Insnar'd with Flow'rs, I fall on Grass.

Mean while the Mind, from pleasure less,
Withdraws into its happiness:
The Mind, that Ocean where each kind
Does streight its own resemblance find;
Yet it creates, transcending these,
Far other worlds, and other Seas;
Annihilating all that's made
To a green Thought in a green Shade.

Andrew Marvell, 'The Garden' (1681)

Contents

Author's Note

My thanks and acknowledgements to the following sources of original publication: The Royal Society for the Protection of Birds and *Birds* magazine for 'Spring Fever'; *Illustrated London News* for 'Home County'; Oxford University Press for 'A Tide in the Affairs'; *The Countryman*, Burford, Oxon, for 'Heath and Home' and 'Damp Humours'; *the Sunday Telegraph* magazine for 'Paper Dreams' and 'Hyde Park; *Good Housekeeping* for 'The Tides of March' and 'The Promised Landscape'; The British Tourist Authority and *In Britain* for 'The Yorkshire Dales'; *Vole* for 'The New Forest', 'After the Elm,' 'Life on Earth' and the articles in Part Five; *New Society* for 'The Green Backlash'; *Harper's & Queen* for 'Oxford: City of Greening Spires'; Century Publishing Company Ltd for the introduction to *The Wild Garden*; Penguin Books Ltd for the introduction to *The Natural History of Selborne* and the introduction to *Landscapes with Figures*; Scolar Press for the introduction to *Gilbert White's Year*; *The Times* for the article on James Fisher, 'Masterful Unravelling' and 'The country Diary'; *Punch* for 'A Mushroom Grew in Berkeley Square'. (Fuller details of first publication are given at the beginning of each piece.)

All the pieces have been slightly amended from their original form, chiefly to avoid overlap, correct errors, remove topical references which are now meaningless and tidy up some of the sloppy writing that can slip in on rushed journalistic schedules. But the judgements in them remain untouched, even where my own opinion has subsequently changed.

Introduction

This book contains a selection of essays and articles on countryside and landscape matters, mostly written during the last ten years. My choice of what to include was governed, in the first instance, simply by what I still liked and felt had stood the test of time: second, and less surely, by a sense of what was representative of different periods in my writing life. The result is something of a mixed bunch, ranging from snatches of autobiography, forays into landscapes both familiar and bizarre, reviews, columns, critical essays and even a smattering of science. I was relieved that in the end some kind of consistent theme – or at least a persistent set of preoccupations – seemed to emerge from the potpourri.

At their root almost all the pieces are worrying away at a single question: why late twentieth-century urban and industrial society should be increasingly drawn to and fascinated by the natural world and by rural landscapes that in their form and use are increasingly alien. For me, this is still an unresolved personal question. I was born in and have lived most of my life in the Chilterns, yet I find it hard to think of myself as 'rural' in any conventional sense. What work I have done on the land has been a matter of leisure not necessity, and I cannot accept many of the social attitudes and habits that are regarded as customary (and perhaps even 'natural') for country dwellers. My education was in philosophy and politics, and my work, first as a teacher and then as a writer, has always been as much connected with metropolitan intellectual life as with my geographical roots. All of which brands me decisively as an 'outsider' to the rural native (and only redeemed, ironically, by a bookish view of natural history which I acquired comparatively recently).

Yet I cannot say that I feel estranged or displaced. Increasingly I feel my writing is a kind of rural work, just as I feel that the widespread modern yearning for a relationship with nature and the land based, not on ownership or labour, but on simple delight and sensual and spiritual renewal, is an authentic search for a modern role for the countryside.

It is not a new search, of course. As far back as Richard Jefferies, for instance (see page 133), writers have wrestled with the difficulties of celebrating natural and rural scenes that were sustained by the blind toil of others. But now the toil is less, and it is nature itself that is being degraded. Our own countryside has become a complicated and powerfully emotive symbol of our precarious life in the world, where we can glimpse some of the diversity and renewal and sense of fittingness increasingly absent from our own lives. That this great repository of values is itself being remorselessly eroded is what makes our concern about its future so great.

I have begun the collection with some pieces on my 'home range' in the Chilterns and East Anglia. Our complex reactions to our native patches show up how facile is a vew of landscape as a purely visual concept. Smells, sounds, childhood associations, echoes of ancient work intertwine (not always harmoniously) with the more tutored insights of human and natural history.

Certainly the conflict between intuition and tuition pervades all our relationships with the countryside, and we have a hard and probably futile struggle trying to advance our understanding of it whilst preserving a vestige of native or natural innocence (if indeed we ever had such a thing). Some writers, like White and, later, John Clare, tried to resolve the conflict by rooting themselves in their aboriginal landscapes. There, at least, new, disruptive knowledge could be kept under control.

Now, we are all connoisseurs of landscape, even if we never leave the living room. We have been educated to such an understanding of the way that landscapes 'work' that even quite unfamiliar places can be comprehensible, and then bewitching. First sights become second nature. When I come, now, down the road from Alton and see the dark bulk of Selborne Hanger swing against the sun, or I rattle over the first cattle grids in the New Forest at Cadnam, I feel a prickle of excitement that is akin to coming home. I have included some accounts of my developing reactions to fond but less familiar landscapes in the Parts Two and Three.

Our responses, of course, are influenced by writers and artists, and the Part Four is concerned with 'country' writers, ancient and modern, and the ways they have informed our perspectives and values. Some would go further and say *formed*, not informed. But White, Clare, Jefferies, *et al* had responses too, and though their attachments are as various as their own lives and local scenes, so many common *kinds* of response have run right through our history – the delight in intricacy and variety, in natural renewal, in the interplay between wildness and cultivation – that it is tempting to think they may be rooted in something deeper than merely fashionable or educated taste.

There is now a developing discipline of landscape research which is looking for scholarly answers to these questions. One school favours the theory of 'prospect and refuge' and proposes that our landscape preferences derive from atavistic biological needs. Another suggests that our favourite landscapes all contain an element of mystery, where 'more information is promised than is actually revealed'. W. G. Hoskins, the father of landscape studies, said much the same thing: 'I expect a landscape to speak to me and to ask questions – or rather to pose problems, which merely pretty scenery does not.'

I suspect that feelings about landscape – personal and public alike – involve both these kinds of response, and much more. Why, for instance, are we so attracted by winding paths and lanes? A track is the primal landscape, the first mark a human being (or any animal) makes on the earth. But why *winding* tracks? Is it simply because 'more information is promised than is actually revealed' at any one moment? Because we enjoy the seeming rightness of a route that follows the natural dips and folds and obstructions of the land? Or because we intuitively know that this is the way that *we* meander, faced with the task of crossing a new space? Ronald Blythe has written: 'What the majority of us celebrate as natives are native improvements. The shapes, colours and scents have an ancestral significance, and what moves us is that the vista does not radiate from some proto-creation like a dawn-stone, but is a series of constructions made by our labouring fathers.'*

I am attracted by the idea that our responses to landscapes are affected by the degree to which we recognize human associations and human handiwork in the patterns on the land; and especially, paradoxically, when those associations and that handiwork appear to join us more closely with the life and work of nature. I have in front of me a copy of John Sell Cotman's painting of Mousehold Heath near Norwich. The picture is dominated by the tracework of paths worn out by centuries of human and animal traffic. They swirl down the hills, broadening, dividing, meeting again. It is exactly the pattern that would be made by a stream finding its own course down the slope; or, more fancifully, like the lines long exposure to weather makes on a face.

Landscapes are a physical record of our history and labour, our inventiveness and sense of community. They are also records of the continuing struggle between private ambition and social need. In this sense they are a kind of common concrete language, and Margaret Drabble has called them a 'link between what we were and what we are'. But we cannot let the definition rest there, caught like a fossil in the rocks. Landscapes are not static. They are owned, worked, changed sometimes by the vitality of the natural world – that supposedly enduring cornerstone – itself. Sometimes they are obliterated altogether. We are not often landscape-makers or owners, and it is rarely in our power to take part in the reconciliation between human control and natural spontaneity that is what we seem to want in our rural surroundings. The question of how the vast bulk of us who feel deeply and organically involved with landscapes and natural life, yet who are estranged from them geographically and socially, can work out a relationship, has only just begun to be explored.

---

* 'An inherited perspective', *From The Headlands,* Chatto & Windus, 1982.

PART ONE

Heartlands

Spring Fever

First published in *Birds*, Spring 1978

I'm afraid it must be a chronic affliction. Every year I fret away the damp and birdless days of early April, wondering if they will ever come back. And every May I wake one morning to a clear sky alive with swifts and martins, and am cured in a minute. It does not last. Come next spring, I am looking out of the window at the chill north-easterlies ruffling the primroses and thinking mournfully about the birds held up on the other side of the Channel, each of us, in our different ways, trapped by our expectations.

We seem to make a more heartfelt response to the coming of spring than any other season. The first green film on the hawthorns, or a swallow on Easter Day, can lift the spirits far more than is explicable by a simple relief that winter is past. Perhaps our biological roots are deeper than we think, and we recognize these natural tokens as part of an annual renewal in which we still share.

When I was at school our talisman was the chiffchaff. For the first few days of the Easter holidays we would comb the woods for them, trying to push our personal first dates further and further back into March. It was about as devout as a game of conkers, and it was only years later that I learned to appreciate the sweet and subtle triumph in that first new voice of spring. The bird that touched me most then – as now – was the swift. But no random swift would do. No precociously early date would make up for a bird in the wrong place at the wrong time. *My* first swift had to fly above a high meadow I crossed on the way to afternoon cricket on the first day of May. I trudged up the hill with my bike, gazing into the air and holding my blazer collar for luck, aching for a glimpse of those careering crescent wings.

Swifts have become as important to us as nightingales were

to the Romantics, but I'm not sure I can fully explain the spell they hold over me. There is, of course, the thrill of their mass chases round the housetops, and the poignancy of their life styles, so completely aerial that a young swift spends three years entirely on the wing (covering 3,000,000 miles) between fledging and first breeding. But the real reasons, what I feel when I see them back again, aren't anything like as rational and objective as this. They have to do with renewal again, and with the extraordinary sense of privilege that comes from having such cryptic, remote birds returning, every year, to spend the best three months of the summer in *our* parish.

Meanwhile, whilst we're waiting, the resident birds make their own welcome diversions. There is a pair of collared doves that appears regularly on our lawn in the first mild days of January. There are mistle thrushes that skirl through the gales of February from the lime trees down the lane, and not long after, the first real dawn chorus. And in early March there is almost always a spell of mild weather that will be all we see of spring for the next four or five weeks. Larks sing, pussy willows buzz with yellow-dusted bees. Last year, I remember, it began at the very start of the month with a day of bizarre manifestations: a brimstone butterfly in the back garden, a frog in the front, and a French partridge, under the cherry tree, that sprinted down the lawn and vanished along our drive.

They carry on the spring, the inexorable thread of new life. Yet on bleak mid-April days, how one longs for the return of the summer birds, for the reassurance that comes from long-awaited arrivals. Our first pair of local swallows always returns at this time, to a site they have clung to with such persistence and magnanimity that it makes you ashamed of all those sceptical proverbs. This solitary pair helps make many people's summers. They nest by the railway station, under a bridge which carries the main line to Euston over a busy road. They have survived not just the traffic but the rebuilding of the bridge, and in the evenings they swoop over the heads of the homebound commuters and fly the 100 yards to the moat of our Norman castle, where their ancestors probably hunted for midges nearly a thousand years ago.

But these swallows are exceptional in moving into their

summer quarters so early. Most other migrants are biding their time near patches of open water, waiting for a change in the weather. Sometimes, when the cold winds hold on beyond the end of April, I have seen gatherings of martins, swifts and swallows so many thousands strong over a nearby reservoir that the surface of the water seemed to be boiling with them. It is a breathtaking sight, but it cannot compare with that moment in early May when the wind veers round to the south, and the birds come home, back to the streets and steeples.

W. H. Hudson once wrote about 'birds at their best'. I think he had in mind these moments when a bird seems to belong utterly to a particular landscape. I remember a wood warbler I saw in a Chiltern beechwood one spring. It was the first warm day of May and you could still see the sky through the thin-leaved lattice of the branches. Primroses were in flower, and blackcaps and garden warblers singing in the undergrowth. And in their midst – the soloist to their chorus – was a single wood warbler, in full tremulous song. It was on a thin beech sapling, not 12 feet from me, and even without binoculars I could see its throat shaking with every note of that falling, clear-water song, and seeming in the filtered sunlight to be the same translucent green as the young beech leaves. A bird at its best, and undeniably in its place.

And with the spring fully settled, I feel a need to see the summer birds 'in their places'. I suppose it is a kind of beating of the bounds, not just of the parish itself, but of my internal map of haunts and memories, a way of confirming the continuity in my own life as much as in the landscape. The track I follow is always the same. I go up the hill to the wood where I searched for chiffchaffs when I was a boy, cross a narrow valley where swallows hawk over a farm pond, and climb to a patch of chalk scrub that is always thronging with warblers. I stay here till dusk. Sometimes a sparrowhawk glides down the valley, sometimes a woodcock on its roding circuit, both, like me, checking out their territories. And high in the night sky, beyond human sight, the parish swifts cruise above the sodium lights, home for the summer.

By a quirk of geography, most of this home range lies not in Hertfordshire, where I was born and live, but just over the border in Buckinghamshire. This creates a problem of identity that is typical of these parts.

Home County

First published as 'Richard Mabey's Hertfordshire' in
Illustrated London News, March 1982

The trouble with Hertfordshire is that it has a low profile and earns low loyalties. There is no quintessential county landscape, no great range of hills or heaths. There is no Hertfordshire cheese, sheep, hot-pot or pudding (though there is Hertfordshire puddingstone, a glacial relic which pops up here and there and consists of a conglomeration of rough stones held together by natural cement). You will need to talk to a life-long inhabitant for first-hand memories of an authentic local industry. Hertfordshirepersons don't even have any oddball qualities for people to make jokes about. The nearest thing to a piece of county mythology I have heard is Bernard Miles's laconic tale of a family tombstone that was 'the finest piece of sharpening stone in all Hertfordshire', which he would relate in a dry and measured accent exactly halfway between Wessex round and Norfolk flat. But then Bernard Miles, I hardly need add, also lived just over the border, in Middlesex.

Having no sharply defined character of its own, Herts is apt to take on the contours and hues of its more distinct neighbours. Much of the south of the county, for instance, seems little more than a dense and busy carapace of north London, whilst the extreme east is as olde-world as Essex. It depends on your point of view. Drive down from the rural north, along the Great North Road through Stevenage, or the Old Roman

Ermine Street through Hoddesdon (now the A10) and Herts appears as a long, low industrial estate, a working suburbia of compact electronics factories, garden centres, office complexes and gravel pits landscaped for anglers and weekend sailors. Wind you way westwards from the North Circular, through Bushey, Oxhey and Chorleywood, and it is a thickening vista of beechwoods and gorse-covered commons.

If you actually live here you may not have a view at all of the county as such. It is hardly firm enough ground to grow roots in. Herts is more a kind of temporary mooring, a place to commute from, to pause in on the way to somewhere else, to leave behind at the end of a working life. Through-traffic has been one of its burdens since prehistoric times. The county's oldest road, the Icknield Way, was in use as the main route between Wessex and the Wash four thousand years ago. It was taken along the chalk ridge on the extreme north-west edge of the county to bypass the densely wooded claylands that covered its centre. Since then Herts has been criss-crossed by the Grand Union Canal, four main railway lines, and bits of five motorways. Most of the proposed sites for the third London Airport have been just a few miles one side or other of its boundary.

All these facilities for hectic toing and froing reflect the looming presence of the capital, which has been the major force in shaping Hertfordshire's character for more than a thousand years. With nothing particular to act as a counter-balance – a coastline, for example, as have those other sub-urban counties, Essex and Kent – London exerts its influence in much the same way as a magnet affects iron filings, giving a slant, a kind of metropolitan restlessness, to everything from house prices to insect life (Herts has more species of flea than any county in England). Looked at the other way, we live at the edge of the capital's shadow, where urban stresses become faint and muddled. The first vague memories of my life are of the grim wartime struggles being acted out to the south, which to my uncomprehending infant eyes seemed more like a circus than a world war. There were distant dog-fights and languid barrage balloons in the day, and searchlights playing about the sky at night. The morning after an air-raid I would toddle out on to the lawn to gather the thin strips of metal foil the bombers had dropped to confuse our radar. They lay amongst the dew and daisies like gossamer. Once a bomb was off-loaded into a nearby field, blowing a chip off our greenhouse wall and leaving a vast crater. For years afterwards I assumed that all the dells and holes with which West Herts is pitted (ancient and innocent marl diggings for the most part) were caused by German bombs.

These are the kinds of incongruity and distortion that London's proximity can nurture. It gives much of the country-side a vulnerable, unsettled look, and encourages the towns to fray at the edges. Hertfordshire is the county where, in the 1920s, a fig tree sprouted out of a tomb in Watford cemetery, and, with a pattern of growth scarcely less probable, the first garden cities were created in Letchworth and Welwyn.

But I am making it sound like so much puddingstone, all quirky lumps set in rather bland dough. Although the constant contrast of old and new, urban and rural, sometimes seems like a huge topographical cartoon – as where the Euston–Manchester Intercity line has to mount a mighty embankment to cross the marshy edges and triple moat of Berkhamsted's Norman castle – it can also be startling enough to make your heart beat faster. Drive into Hemel Hempstead New Town on the A41 in mid-May, and look at the golden blaze of Boxmoor's buttercup meadows wedged between road and railway. Or out of Baldock on a winter's afternoon, up the graciously broad medieval market street, east into the Icknield Way, past the Victorian maltings on your left, to find yourself, suddenly and unexpectedly, in a vast East Anglian vista of limitless chalky fields, shining as the low sun is reflected off flints and furrows.

This point is one of the gateways through Hertfordshire's chief internal boundary, between the light, chalky soils of the north and east, and the heavier clays of the south and west. The arable fields that stretch for miles around Royston and Buntingford and into Cambridgeshire and Essex, with scarcely a hedge or bank between them, are the latest developments in a pattern of agriculture that was set by neolithic farmers. Since the forest was easier to clear on the light soils than on the clay, this is where most of the major early settlements clustered and grew. By Domesday the pattern was fixed: 'woodlands with swine' are concentrated in the west and 'ploughteams' in the north and east. If the woodland settlements meant a pastoral economy with a multitude of scattered, self-sufficient small-holdings, the cornlands were the strongholds of the open field system and of highly organized and cooperative nucleated villages. These, sadly, were all too vulnerable to human disease and crop failure, and to the bureaucratic 'improvements' of Parliamentary Enclosure during the eighteenth and nineteenth centuries. The rationalized landscape of rectangular fields and dead straight roads that resulted led inevitably to the huge, hedgeless prairies and similarly huge machines that are the current fashion in arable organization.

As a landscape it is too airy to be oppressive, but I find it lonely as well as featureless, and full of melancholy echoes. This is not the first time these now very open fields have been drained of people. The region is littered with the sites of deserted medieval villages, abandoned during prolonged periods of bad harvest or plague. On an inside wall of the great tower of St Mary's Church in Ashwell (where the open field system survived into the twentieth century) an anonymous reporter has scratched a bleak graffito about the march of the Black Death. It is as chilling a cry out of the past as I have ever read: '1350, wretched, wild, distracted. The dregs of the mob alone survive to tell the tale. At the end of the second [outbreak of plague] was a mighty wind. St Maurus thunders in all the world.'

Villages were also commonly deserted or rearranged because of the whims of 'improving' landowners, and an outlandish example of this is Ayot St Lawrence, probably Hertfordshire's best-known village because of its association with Bernard Shaw. In 1778 Sir Lionel Lyte, director of the Bank of England, London tobacconist and local squire, decided to pull down the village's modest medieval church and build something more in keeping with the spirit of the age. The Bishop stopped him before he had finished demolishing old St Lawrence, but Lyte continued with his other plans and as a result there now stands on the edge of this tiny village a large and stunning Palladian Temple. It was – and is – a working folly, used for worship, though 'the unfortunate villagers had to make a wide detour, approaching the building from the back and entering by a side door so as not to spoil the view from the House.'

Shaw himself regarded it as a monstrosity, though his own piece of early 20th C Det. ('Shaw's Corner') is hardly an architectural jewel. GBS's somewhat churlish tastes, however, received their comeuppance at the hands of Hertfordshire's *genius loci*. It is a bizarre story. In 1931 Shaw began an acrimonious correspondence with Islington Council over their refuse tip at Wheathampstead, which is just one mile, as the wind blows, from Ayot. Shaw quoted Exodus on plagues of flies, and compared the smoking tip to the volcano of Stromboli. The council denied his charges. The tip, meanwhile, apparently favouring Judges 12 ('out of the strong shall come forth sweetness') as its text, was taking matters into its own hands, and the following year an apple tree of prolific blossom and unknown pedigree grew out of Islington's rubbish. In 1936 it produced one single, gigantic fruit weighing a pound and a half, which Shaw's cook tricked him into eating in a stew. After the war, grafts from this wilding were grown successfully on a commercial scale, and are still sometimes known as Shaw's Pippin.

Ayot, strictly, is over the Hitchin–Hertford line and in the county's western woodland zone. This is my own patch of Herts, especially where the claylands merge with the Chilterns in the extreme west. I find it a very agreeable countryside, compact and manageable but always surprising. It is a landscape of dips and folds, ponds and Ends, and straggling commons that have probably never been enclosed since they were first grazed in the Iron Age. Above all there are the woods. Too many have become uniform smudges of conifer for my taste, but there aren't many high places where you can't stand amongst trees and look at a continuous line of woodland on the next scarp. In autumn they are as colourful as the woodlands of the Weald. Beech is both wild and planted, but there is cherry, field maple and hornbeam in abundance too, mottling the beech's rusts and coppers with crimson, orange and lemon in autumn.

One of the most striking woods – and by now one of the most familiar in Britain – is the beech hanger that sweeps down the hill behind the much-filmed village of Aldbury, with its commuters' cottages clustered round pond and green and stocks. There is also a mansion called Stocks in the village, where the Playboy Club's Bunny Girls used to be trained. It isn't, I should hastily add, named after the local bondage instrument, but after the old word for an area of stumps, or cleared woodland. And this, really, is the key to the landscape of West Herts. It was cleared and enclosed by individual effort direct from the forest. Hence the tangle of narrow, banked lanes and paths joining isolated farmhouses, the greens that served as night-time refuges for stock or as grazing stations along droveways, and the continuously changing mosaic of wood and clearing.

It was this personalized mixture that so moved Cobbett when he rode between Redbourn and Hemel Hempstead in 1822 '. . . the sort of corn, the sort of underwood and timber, the shape and size of the fields, the height of the hedgerows, the height of the trees, all continually varying. Talk of *pleasure-grounds* indeed! What that man ever invented, under the name of pleasure-grounds, can equal these fields in Hertfordshire?' So close were these do-it-yourself landscapes to the ideal of pastoral wilderness that when Capability Brown came to create 'landskip' parks at Ashridge, Beechwood, Digswell, Moor Park and Youngsbury, he remarked of one of them, 'Nature has done so much, little was wanting, but enlarging the River.'

I suspect both Brown and Cobbett would be shocked at the degree to which the variety that so impressed them has been levelled down. Yet a streak of wildness still plays across these western frontier lands. At the beginning of the century much of this western protuberance of Herts was owned by the Rothschilds. They bought Tring Park in 1786, and many of the villages round about are graced by the distinctive gabled cottages they built for their workers. But the Rothschilds were eccentric explorers and animal collectors as well as farmers and financiers. One was famous for riding about Tring in a cart drawn by zebras, and dotting the Park with enclosures full of exotic animals. But the enclosures weren't quite secure enough. Rothschild's edible dormouse, the glis-glis, now spends the winters snoozing in local lofts, and the summers munching the tops off beech saplings. Rothschild's giant catfish, introduced from central Europe, still haunt the depths of Tring Reservoirs, which, with true Herts contrariness, were the first wholly man-made lakes to be declared a National Nature Reserve.

Even the capital of the region, the elegant cathedral city of St Albans, has pagan leanings. St Albans was founded in AD 950 by the abbot Wulsin, on the site of the Roman town of Verulamium. But before that the area was a stronghold of a tribe of Belgic Celts known as the Catuvellauni. They lived in Prae Wood, about a mile west of the present city, and by all accounts were wealthy and artistic, and pioneers of benign alternative technologies. They fought off the Roman chariots with an awesome (and still surviving) system of 40-foot-deep ditches, but were finally beaten in 54 BC. It's encouraging to see that their spiritual ancestors have been gaining ground recently against the vestiges of Roman authoritarianism. 'Snorbens', as the new Herts Celts call their city, quite properly remembering their roots are pre-Christian, is a bright and innovative community, full of peace groups, poets, live-music pubs and all manner of modern friends of the earth. This was the birthplace of the wood-burning stove revival and the Campaign for Real Ale, but it is saved from being too folksily precious by the best Chinese and Indian take-aways in the area. It even has a thoroughgoing Catuvellaunian in the shape of Ginger Mills, the wildman of St Albans, who lives in a van at the edge of the city and amazes the earnest brass-rubbing tourists throughout the summer. My friend Jeff Cloves wrote a broadsheet poem about 'this spangled aboriginal stomping among the brittle relics of Centurions and Abbots', and says that 'Ginge, like the true artist he is, was buying copies from me at a tanner and selling them for two bob.'

This area of Herts seems always to have been environmentally conscious, and it was an upsurge of concern amongst the urban middle class that led to the saving of much of the commonland in the west of the county, typified by the famous estates of Ashridge (now owned by the National Trust). By the middle of the nineteenth-century Parliamentary Enclosure had put paid to many commons at Watford, Bushey, Barnet, and Wigginton, but it was becoming clear that the remainder had a vital role to play as places for the recreation of the new urban multitudes. So when Lord Brownlow rather dubiously fenced off 400 acres of Berkhamsted Common it was not so much the dispossessed graziers who fought back as the new commuters, led by Augustus Smith, Lord of the Scilly Isles. In March 1866 he imported a gang of 130 London navvies, who marched up from the station and tore down the 3 miles of iron railings. There followed a great open-air celebration by the townspeople, a fifteen-verse ballad in *Punch*, a law suit for damages by Brownlow, and an immediate and successful counter suit for illegal enclosure by Smith. It was a famous and decisive victory and it subsequently became increasingly difficult to enclose commons near towns. Hertfordshire has 186 registered commons and village greens, of enormous variety. Berkhamsted Common, with its ancient pollard beeches and sweeps of birch and gorse, is one of the largest in the Home Counties. Chipperfield has a cricket pitch set in a holly wood. Roughdown and Sheethanger Commons, at Hemel Hempstead, are on an outcrop of chalk, and support not just a roller-coaster of a golf course, but a flock of Soay sheep, which graze amongst wild orchids within sight of the John Dickinson paper factory.

So many of Hertfordshire's commons have courses that golf, with its suburban social codes and skills, might be reckoned the county sport – were it not for the extraordinary, burgeoning popularity of horse-riding. In many of the wealthier areas, round Flaunden, Bovingdon and Little Gaddesden, for instance, it's believed that the population of ponies now exceeds that of people. Along with them has come a new (and not always welcome) landscape of oil-barrel jumps and bare, fenced fields around the village perimeters.

But all these developments are a kind of apotheosis of the Hertfordshire paradox. A split-level house amongst the trees near a fairway, a pony and a paddock for the children, a good motorway link with London – this, for an increasing number of people, is the recipe for the Good Life.

It had all been anticipated, of course. In the late eighteenth and early nineteenth century *nouveau riche* industrialists and merchants chose Hertfordshire as a convenient retreat from the City. And by 1848, what is now the Lea Valley Park was already a recreation area for the metropolis. One guidebook (to Rye House, in the Valley) commented that 'so numerous have been the visitors to this pleasant place, that the Directors of the Great Eastern Railway Company have erected a station within a few yards of the spot.' The railway companies bowed gratefully to the growing popularity of the county, began buying development land along their extending lines, and by 1920 were set to create the first generation of commuters. 'The song of the nightingales for which the neighbourhood is renowned . . .' ran a Metropolitan Railway Company advert in 1920, 'the network of translucent rivers traversing the peaceful valley render Rickmansworth a Mecca to the city man pining for the country and pure air.'

Ebenezer Howards's garden cities at Letchworth and Welwyn were based on the same dream, and if they seem unexceptional now, it is partly because their curving, tree-lined roads and wide verges have become routine features of up-market suburban development; and partly because they gave birth in their turn to the feckless and artificially grafted new towns at Hemel Hempstead, Hatfield and Stevenage. At their worst, these are as shabby and heartless as inner-city tower blocks, a cheapskate New Jerusalem to have offered London's overspill. But at their best they can have moments of unexpected charm, and are the one area where you may finally pin down Hertfordshire's amorphous county spirit. E. M. Forster called the county 'England meditative'. In modern jargon I suppose we might say that is was 'soft' – low on definition, open to impression. So you can move about in these fringelands, neither town nor country, and invent a personal county identity as you go. You might hear medieval carols ringing around a pedestrian precinct; or watch a deer scuttle out of a villa garden in Sunnyside Avenue. This is the animal that gave the county its name, after all, though now, of course, it's not the Royal red beast, but the diminutive muntjac that has spread from Knebworth, where they have a rock-music festival next to the deer park.

A Tide in the Affairs

First published in *Places*, edited by Ronald Blythe,
Oxford University Press, 1981

I was nearly 18 before I succeeded in getting as far north as the
Norfolk coast. One summer a friend whose father had a
converted lifeboat moored at Blakeney invited a group of us to
spend a few days there. We went up in his Land Rover, ten of
us, scrabbling about in the back like overexcited puppies. For all
of us, East Anglia was something of an unknown quantity. It
had a reputation as a bit of an outback, on the way to nowhere,
and as its prospects began to unfold before us north of New-
market, it looked like a very strange country indeed. American
bomber bases glinted ominously in distant heaths. Asparagus
grew in sandy fields. The roads were lined with stunted pine
windbreaks, unlike any hedges we had ever seen. Then,
further on, there were no margins at all, and the great washes
of sugar beet and barley broke abruptly against the flint
walls of medieval churches. When we swung into the long
straight reach of the Icknield Way, north of Brandon, Justin,
our driver and host, sensing our excitement but also aware of
the responsibility of having such a gathering of greenhorns
in his charge, hunched down towards the dashboard and
showed us how he could change into four-wheel drive with
his foot.

We saw more kicking out – and the same mixture of nonchalance and authority – that evening in a Blakeney pub. One
of the regulars was Crow, a ruddy-faced village elder, yarner
and Jack-of-all-trades, whom we came to adulate in a rather
silly way as a local 'character'. He, of course, made merciless
fun of us by acting out the role for all his worth. That night he
showed us a natty trick he had with the bar skittles. He
would aim the ball somewhere between the door-knob and
the photograph of the pre-war lifeboat crew that hung on the
wall, and on the backswing give it a flick with his foot that

made it swoop round and knock every skittle flat. Crow was in his late 50s then, the same age as most of the lifeboatmen in the photo. The picture had been taken after a momentous rescue in which conditions had been so terrible that the men's hands had been frozen solid to the oars. Norfolk, that evening, looked like a place where one might have to flex all manner of undiscovered muscles.

Yet even on those first visits the place sounded old chords. It was the first time I had gone tribal since I was a child in the early fifties. I was with another gang then and we spent our school holidays in the grounds of a demolished eighteenth-century mansion behind our road. We went out there first thing, built camps up trees and in holes in the ground, churned milk on upturned bicycles, baked potatoes in wood fires, fought off invaders from the council estate on the far side of the park, and then went home for tea. We used it as our common, and always referred to it, rather imperiously, as 'The Field'. Everywhere else, just as airily, was 'Up the Top'. And up the top, in ecstatic daydreaming on the hills to the south of our road, was where I spent most of the remainder of my youth. It was a patch of country that I clung to like a secret code, full of touchstones and private vistas that had to be visited in a precise and rigid sequence. It was right enough for a brooding adolescent, but when Norfolk arrived I was glad to be back with some company again, and with a landscape that seemed to have some of the perennial new-mintedness of those childhood mornings in 'The Field'.

We spent that first Norfolk night, as we were to spend many more in the years to come, crammed into the eccentric cavities of the old lifeboat (which was called, for reasons beyond any fathoming, *Dilemma X*). The lucky few had bunks, the rest of us found what spaces we could under tables and in the wheelhouse. In the morning I wriggled stiffly out of my own cranny near the bilges, found a porthole, and looked out on the sight that has kept me in thrall to this coastline ever since: a high tide swirling in over a mile of saltmarsh and lapping the concrete quay where we were moored. There was not a single point of stillness. Terns hovered above the water and spikes of sea-lavender bent and bounced under the tide-race. Even the mud was alive, and slid out of the receding water with the moist shine of a new-born animal.

Saltmarshes don't fit into our conventional views about landscape. They are neither sea nor dry land. Most of the time they have the comfortably timeless look of old pastureland, yet twice a day they are reshaped by the sea. The men who go out on them to dig for lugworm and mussels also live odd hybrid existences, hunter-gathering in season, odd-jobbing on farms and gardens in the summer. They use the language of land-workers to describe the mudflats, and talk of fields and valleys and ditches; yet they know that no tractor could drag them out if they were caught by tides that come in faster than a person can walk.

The local ferrymen showed their indifference to the shifting contours of Blakeney Channel by bringing in their boats at the lowest possible water, holding the tiller with one hand and rolling a cigarette ('wibbling' they called it) with the other. We were altogether more timid when it came to the sea, and one trip up the spout on *Dilemma* per visit was quite enough. Even then we didn't venture out to the open sea, but to the Pit, a natural haven formed and sheltered by the long shingle spit known as Blakeney Point.

The Point was an enchanted oasis of lagoons and shifting sand-dunes, where seals basked and the air was full of the clamour of oyster-catchers and redshank. Even when rain hung over the mainland this 3-mile-long peninsula often lay under its own mysteriously clear strip of blue sky. It was our Coral Island, and on hot days I can still conjure up the coconut and honey scent of the sea-pinks and tree lupins. (Once or twice, walking over the marshes at nearby Stiffkey, I have seen a true mirage of the Point. It floated high above the horizon, stretched by the heat haze so that its dunes looked like the walls of a Moorish castle.) When the tide went out it left little pools, not more than 2 or 3 feet deep, and warm enough to doze in. Occasionally we would see a great flock of terns swirling like ticker-tape above one of these pools, and raining down after the shoal of whitebait that had been stranded there. We never bothered to try and catch fish ourselves, but we grubbed for cockles and cooked bundles of marsh samphire (wrapped in silver foil – we were no purists) over driftwood fires.

But though we thought sometimes of spending whole days and nights out there, curled up under the dunes, the fantasy of being castaways was never strong enough to keep us from the sociable pleasures of the mainland in the evenings. So when the tide was right we would row back to *Dilemma*, on to the flats on the landward side of the Pit and then walk to the pub at Morston across a mile of glassy mud and rickety plank bridges, with black mud squirting between our toes. It was a hilarious, slithery journey even in the daylight, and how we used to make it back after closing time I do not know. Justin, never one to shirk his captain's responsibilities, wouldn't allow us to use torches in case we dropped them and fell away ourselves with night blindness (some of the creeks under those bridges were 10 feet deep). So if there was no moon the only light was the phosphorescence that rippled about our feet as we splashed into the shallow water. Sometimes we could see our last footprints glowing for a brief instant in the damp sand behind us, as long-lived a trace as anyone leaves here. I learned much later that it was partly these marsh-lights that Justin thought had given samphire, the plant which grew in these muds, its name. Never having had a reason to see the word written, he thought it was 'sand-fire'.

In wintertime the Point was too wild and wind-torn for our tastes, but we still haunted these marshes north of Morston, and took long, tacking walks along the sea-walls. At New Year the sky here is often the purest, sharpest blue, and is etched with vast flights of wintering birds – wild swans, wigeon, flocks of waders swirling like smoke over the distant slack water with their pale underwings flashing in the sun as they turn.

I've never understood those who find marshes desolate places. They can be remorselessly hard, especially in winter, but they are never oppressive. They are too open for that. If you look east or west along these flats you can sometimes see for a dozen miles, up to the edge of the Wash, if you are lucky. The view would swallow you if it were not for the rim of the sea itself. It is a shifting edge, but it puts a comforting limit to things. On the tideline, you know where you are. Stand by it and look due north and there is nothing between you and the Arctic Circle. The North Sea here is as dark as anywhere in Britain, and the locals still often refer to it by its stark ancient name, the German Ocean.

Yet turn round and look inland and you could be in the Chilterns. In the mile or so that lies between the sea and the coast-road the marshes gradually assemble themselves. Nearest you are the bare sands and the plastic, shifting muds; then the pastel wash of the first plants, the silver wormwood and lilac sea-lavenders; then the claimed land locked up behind the sea-walls; and finally, backed up against the low swell of the coastal hills, the little villages with their mighty churches, as compact and bright as if they were tucked in a secure inland valley.

It's hard to feel lonely where there is a tide. Whatever else it may be, it is reliable. A tide will come in, always more or less on time, and always, eventually, recede. The signs the spent water leaves on the sand and mudflats are like vanishing footprints. They are soft-edged, fleeting, curiously tidy. Perhaps it is this husbanding by the sea that gives marshy landscapes what affinities they have with more slowly moulded sceneries inland. It is as if a whole round of seasons – or a whole generation of farming – were enacted twice a day.

Every few years the sea breaks in more savagely, but even then the changes are transient. Early in 1976 a great storm breached sea-walls right along the coast and all the shore line habitats – beaches, sand, mudflats, saltings – were thrown together in a mad jumble. The sea sprayed tongues of shingle far into the marsh and hollowed out muddy pools in the middle of the beach. In many places the rows of sea-blite bushes that grow along the margin between beach and mud were completely buried by shingle. But by August that year their shoots had already started to reappear above the surface. I dug down below one of these new sprigs, down to the old and already decaying parent plants, and saw the new shoots, pallid but indomitable, pushing their way up through more than 2 feet of heavy pebbles.

These harsh conditions demand a measure of adaptability from everything that lives here. Once or twice a year, when high spring tides are boosted by north-easterly winds, the seaward edge of Blakeney floods. In the summer everyone gathers round the quay to see the tide in, and it becomes a kind of coastal village green. The car park attendant's booth bobs free and floats off, the bus stop is moved, and as the water starts lapping the steps of the knitwear store in the High Street, the more adventurous boat-people go shopping in their tenders. This narrow street is steep enough to give a view over the whole quay and out into the Pit, and you can see how the tide drives everything remorselessly before it – spectators, cars, boats and all – like flecks of spindrift on the shore. When Blakeney Channel was wider and the quay used commercially, the cargoes had to be edged down this slope in carts braked by backward-facing horses. Steep land, high water: the influence of the elements of a landscape can be ineluctable. I've watched a bulldozer, clearing up flotsam after one of these flood tides, run gently out of control down the hill and over the edge of the quay. And once, when we were trundling a piano down the street to the pub, it began to move so fast that the wheels glowed hot and hissed in the puddles.

The tribe has broken up now and its members gone their separate ways, and when I come back to this stretch of Norfolk I am usually by myself. But the marsh landscapes are as familiar company as they ever were. I still follow the old route up – past the airfields and squat pines, along the road from Fakenham that edges, maddeningly slowly, towards the coast. Then through the gorse and heather of Salthouse Heath, that lies on a ridge of sandy gravels dumped here by the last ice-sheet. You see the first glint of water, then as you tip sharply down through the narrow strip of arable fields, the marsh suddenly fills the whole horizon, criss-crossed with silver dykes. You feel age and time falling away. Where you stand was the coastline five hundred years ago. What you are looking at now is a sight that has never been seen exactly so before, nor ever will be again.

I drive as fast as I dare to Morston, kick off my shoes and run out over the mud towards that thin blue line that hangs over the tide's edge, and wonder why I have ever left.

PART TWO

Landscapes

My attachment to the north Norfolk coast turned gradually into a fascination with East Anglia as a whole, and I realized how slanderous was the popular view of the region as a place unremittingly flat, monotonous and private. I began to know parts of Suffolk as well as Norfolk, and wrote my very first landscape portrait about a habitat that both counties shared, the heathlands. Much of it is too local and technical to repeat here, and the remainder strikes me now as too contrived by half. But I must confess to a special affection for this first amateur shot at catching a genius loci, and hope that will excuse the reprinting of some excerpts here.

Heath and Home

First published in *The Countryman*, June 1970

I was initiated into the peculiar magic of the East Anglian heathlands in the course of a single, blazing week one June. It began when I glimpsed my first nightjar floating over the plains of grass, bracken and ancient thorn that roll down to the marshes at Walberswick. A few days later I sat mesmerized between two duelling nightingales on Salthouse Heath on the Norfolk coast. Finally, 50 miles to the south – I could have been 200 to the north – I was hooked completely and irrevocably by the sound of curlews over the heathery plains of Cavenham Heath, just one mile from the A11. . . .

It is a curious obsession, because heaths are hardly the most hospitable of habitats. In winter, when the bracken is starched with frost, they can be forbiddingly spartan places. In high summer the air is heavy with acrid powder flaking off the parched black branches of the furze. Insects drift over you like pollen. Walk about to breathe more easily and you must still cast a wary downward eye for adders.

Yet heaths have a sombre and primitive charm. Thomas Hardy seemed to feel this about his native Egdon, which he described as 'singularly colossal and mysterious in its swarthy monotony'. He saw a landscape more in harmony with the ups and downs of human experience than a pretentious beauty spot could ever be: 'It had a lonely face, suggesting tragic possibilities.'

To a biologist a heath is more precisely definable. One dictionary describes it as 'an area of poor acid soil, usually sandy or gravelly, often dominated by low-growing ericaceous shrubs, especially heather'. Even in East Anglia an enormous range of habitats is covered by this definition: the pine heaths round Thetford, the gorse and broom sheepwalks near Aldeburgh, the bracken sweeps of Lakenheath and Wangford Warrens, and the damp, boggy commons of north-west Norfolk.

But where does true heathland end and scrub or 'waste' begin? You don't need to be an ecologist to sense there is a difference, and it is the way that heathland's special characteristics mesh so fittingly together that gives them their special flavour.

At the most physical level you experience their curious climatic behaviour. Every change in the weather seems to be exaggerated. With no tall trees to act as windbreaks, the arrival of a stiff breeze can cause the temperature to drop dramatically in minutes. On still summer days the absence of shade allows the pockets of air trapped between bushes to heat up to as much as 5°C above the temperature of adjoining woodland. Even the ground warms up quickly, as the dry sandy soil has little more than a third of the specific gravity of damp humus. And if you walk between the sun and a thick bank of broom, gorse and lupin, you can feel the heat reflected off the blossoms.

You do not stride about on heaths as you do on downs. Every signal from your surroundings tells you to amble, dither, rest more often than is needed. And it is when you are still that you realize that a sort of skulking immobility is a major part of the personality of these places. No other environment has quite this aura. In a wood every step opens up new horizons and perspectives. The patterns of light and structure change with your position. There is, too, a sense of constant motion above you, of the leaf canopy and of the birds in it.

Even in a marsh there is a feeling of openness and animation. Your eye, having no solid landmark to fix on, is constantly searching and scanning. This, together with the tremulous effect of the wind on the surface vegetation, can make a marsh appear to be precariously floating on a thin film of liquid – which, I suppose, it nearly is. But a heath is sullen and inert. Nothing moves. The stunted shrubs are as solid as primitive earthworks. The whole landscape seems like some gigantic fossil, the frozen, strewn relics of a more fertile habitat.

In one sense, of course, this is exactly what heaths are. Most were formed by the extensive felling and burning of the forest cover. In areas where the soil is naturally light and sandy the resultant lack of new humus and of protection from the weather has made it difficult for the more luxuriant plants to re-establish themselves. So the typical heathland flora has moved in: tough, stunted, springy plants, resistant to wind and able to survive on next to no moisture. But on the better soils heaths are unstable and, if undisturbed, rapidly develop into scrub and eventually woodland. So fire, a constant companion of dry and brittle places, is not wholly an enemy of the heaths. Without occasional burning few would survive . . . .

If a kind of becalmed scruffiness is one of the essential features of a heath it is also the one that seems most suited to its inhabitants. It is remarkable how the heathland birds, in particular, match the mood of their surroundings as accurately as actors responding to a vivid set. There is not much of the restless toing and froing you see in the hedgerows. Birds glower invisibly in the densest thickets. Yellowhammers buzz on the extremities of bushes like over-ripe pods. Tree pipits detach themselves from the frieze, labour awkwardly upwards and then plunge down again – the abandoned, mannered dive of a shot bird in a Victorian print. The heath drones on around them: turtle doves purr, whitethroats grate. A grasshopper warbler reels interminably from the heart of a gorse bush, its head turning from side to side as it pours out the sound like an intangible cloud around the bush.

Only the nightingale's song seems out of keeping with these withered calls, and yet the bird unquestionably has a heathland style. There is the elusive way the song glides into your awareness; the secret song-perch inside an impenetrably thick but conspicuous bush. All the best nightingales I have heard in East Anglia have chosen a natural amphitheatre for their performances (unless, that is, I was unconsciously choosing one to listen from). I have heard them in dense currant scrub round a Breckland pond, singing against the howl of Phantoms from Lakenheath Air Base; in the bushes by a solitary tennis court on Southwold Common; and in steep barrows of blackthorn and chrome-yellow broom round an old gun-site on Aldringham Walks, so hot in the June sun that I could barely sit on it . . . .

But it is on warm June evenings that the heath comes into its own. I look forward all year to visiting the East Anglian heaths at this time, and to the thrill of hearing the nightjars again – birds that seem the very personification of the heath. The light drains quickly in these parts, and by half-past nine, so does your sense of distance. There seems no order or direction to the lumpy plain in front of you. Extraordinary grunts and squeals start up in the undergrowth. A woodcock lumbers overhead on its roding circuit, an archaic log of a bird, its wingbeats so slight that you wonder how it stays in the air.

A few minutes later the first nightjar begins. At first you cannot place the source of the churring. You turn, trying to narrow the segment from which the sound is coming. Then, quite suddenly, it stops. A branch seems to break free from one of the trees and float towards you, narrow wings arched high over the back, bouncing like a kite tugged by a child. Nightjars seem quite unperturbed by man and will fly so inquisitively close to you that you can see their gaping mouths and white wing-spots. Once, just behind Minsmere, I heard a nightjar and a nightingale singing together from the same thicket – the nightjar on a dead branch at the top, the nightingale in the blackthorn just a few feet below him. It was an unforgettable coloratura duet, with each bird seemingly spurred on by the other, until the whole heath rang with their songs.

But then, as Hardy argues at the beginning of *The Return of the Native*, bleakness never was an adequate description of heathland, when it was capable of being 'majestic without severity, impressive without showiness, emphatic in its admonitions, grand in its simplicity'.

Paper Dreams

1981, reproduced by permission of
Sunday Telegraph magazine

It was the East Anglian interior (what they call 'High Suffolk') that was the greatest revelation. Despite the vast agricultural changes of the last hundred years, the skeleton of its earlier landscapes, an intricate network of immense boundary banks, green lanes and remote woods, was still astonishingly intact.

Ancient Suffolk proved to be as indelibly engraved on maps as on the land, and I soon became a compulsive mapworm. Whenever I was unable to be out East myself, I would browse endlessly over the Ordnance Survey sheets, plotting walks, trying to imagine the shape and character of unknown, unvisited corners, and sometimes just taking a sheer impractical delight in the abstracted patterns on the map.

There were some powerfully evocative patches. The latticework of lanes and contour lines around Rattlesden and Poystreet Green reminded me of the bumpy surfaces of a leaded window and I was sure that if I ever saw it first-hand, the landscape would have just the same capricious pattern of light and shade. Further east was the lonely Saints' country, south of Bungay, where thirteen saintly parishes – including eight different South Elmhams – were threaded together by the yellow byroads like a melancholy concrete poem.

I began to understand what had moved Edward Thomas to write the second of his 'Household Poems', just before he left for the front in 1916. He was teaching map-reading in Essex at the time, and was so entranced by the field and village names on the local Ordnance Survey sheets – 'Wingle Tye and Margaretting Tye, and Skreen, Gooshays, and Cockerells' – that he felt they were the present he would most like to leave his son.

I was just as captivated by the place names of my more northerly corner of East Anglia: Maggotbox and Poppylots, and Mellis, Occold and Rishangles. Why was there another Gretna Green, by a medieval priory just outside Eye? What had happened at High Wrong Corner near Thetford and, not many miles away, induced the normally unsentimental North-folk to honour a patch of damp scrub by a field dyke with the name of Shropham Tuzzy Muzzy?

There are answers, of course, and just occasionally some of this incidental poetry is apt to disappear when you visit places in the flesh. But the sense maps give of being clues to endless layers of historical riddles is their most compelling feature, even when you are looking at quite straightforward information. On the most popular maps, the 1:50,000 series, you can uncover old ridgeways, new footpaths, icehouses and dove-cotes, battlefields, burial mounds, mills and mines, quarries and gorges, where rivers begin and where they can be forded. On larger maps, such as the 1:25,000 series, you can trace the boundaries not just of your own parish but of individual fields, and see whether these are marked by dykes or shelter belts. On the 1:10,000 maps (roughly 6 inches to a mile) even individual trees are sometimes marked.

As well as placing all these features, maps give them names. And the names have meanings which are related to the place – either as it is, or as it was. Go back 150 years (this is the kind of time travel you can do with maps) and you may find the wood that gave a village name the suffix 'holt', or the common pasture that has given a housing estate the incongruous label of 'green'. Sometimes the stories behind the names turn out to be wonderfully convoluted. When the 1803 Enclosure Map for Donnington in Buckinghamshire was being scanned recently it was found to show a streamside plot called Frogcup Meadow. Although there no longer appears to be a parish called Donnington, this is superficially no more or less cryptic than most nineteenth-century field names. But a sharp-witted historical ecologist realized that 'frogcup' could well be what a city surveyor, unused to Bucks. dialects, might make of the local name for that rare and beautiful water-meadow flower, the snakeshead fritillary. This has been variously written down as crawcup, crowcup, fro'cup and frockup (and take your pick as to whether this last one means frock-cup or frock-up). But Vale of Aylesbury citizens who could remember where and when the flower grew locally insist that the correct rendering is *frawcup*. This is the local, inverted pronunciation of Ford-cup – the flower that grew most plentifully in the hamlet of Ford. Ford is next to a village now called Dinton, which was presumably Donnington. It is also the site of a meadow in which fritillaries could be found right up until the 1950s, when it was ploughed for the first time. The field boundaries and stream courses on the modern OS and 1803 maps match up exactly and show that this plant, which now occurs in only a score of old hayfields in the whole of England, had grown at this one site for at least 150 years.

The early nineteenth-century Enclosure Maps and the Tithe Apportionment maps that were produced at about the same time are the largest and most meticulous charts that still survive from this period. They were hand-drawn on fabric or parchment, and it was unusual for more than one or two copies to be made. They are sometimes kept in vicarages, but most have now been transferred to various public record offices. I can remember my first glimpse of our local Tithe Map in the Herts. Record Office. It was all of 6 feet long, and you had to view it piece by piece, holding down the unrolled sections with polished stones.

I'm sure this map's size had something to do with its impact. So did its accuracy and neatness. But what touched me most of all was its intimacy. This was no piece of impersonal surveying. One hundred and fifty years ago a man had tramped round my own favourite woods and fields, and in a tidy copperplate hand had marked in their names and shapes and eccentricities in a way that made them instantly recognizable.

The hand-drawn Tithe Maps are a reminder that maps are made by people, at particular moments in history and often for quite particular purposes. For the county of Suffolk, the first comprehensive map was produced by Joseph Hodskinson in 1783. This was fifty years before the OS began introducing more rigorous survey techniques, but the map is very accurate, and its distances are rarely more than 3 per cent out. It won Hodskinson the praise of the agricultural reformer Arthur Young (who lived near Bury St Edmunds) and a gold medal from the Royal Society for the Encouragement of Arts, Manufacture and Commerce.

The original proposals were first published in 1776, so the whole project took seven years to complete. This is a long while compared with most eighteenth-century maps, and was probably connected with the fact that the surveying and printing had to be paid for by advance subscriptions. The conditions are set out in the 'Proposals', and include an undertaking that on the payment of a one-guinea subscription fee 'The Noblemen's and Gentlemen's Names shall be engraved at their Seats on the Map . . . as well as the Number of Maps they subscribe for . . . .'

And there they are, making collectively what amounts to the first vanity advertisement for some now very familiar stately homes: Earl Cornwallis at West Stow, Richard Savage Lloyd at Hintlesham Hall, the Earl of Bristol at Ickworth, down to Arthur Young himself and the thinly inked garden of one Rev. Nicholas Bacon. Heveningham Hall, the seat of William Gerrard Vanneck, looks especially resplendent. The grounds had been landscaped by Capability Brown just the previous year and great attention has been paid to the drawing of the new lakes, islands and carriage drives.

It's no wonder that the large estates are one of Hodskinson's most painstaking and detailed features: putting someone quite literally on the map is one of the most convincing (and rewarding) forms of flattery. The need to attract subscriptions probably also accounts for the conspicuous care which has been taken over the depiction of the county's commons. The last quarter of the eighteenth-century was a time when Enclosure by Parliamentary Award was gathering pace across England. But in the eastern counties most of the open arable fields had been enclosed piecemeal in medieval times, and agricultural improvers had to concentrate their attention on appropriating common pastures, heaths, peat-fens and woods. Any map which detailed these areas (and Arthur Young believed there were 100,000 acres of such 'waste' land in Suffolk) would be of the greatest interest to ambitious landlords.

The highlighting of the commons could hardly be called bias. But it's an instance of the way that the social functions of maps can affect their emphases. The fact is that maps show not just what is 'there', but also the outlines of their makers' social and intellectual landscapes. Although they use naturalistic codes ('outdoor' colours, miniaturized windmills and churches, for example), maps are necessarily selective. No map smaller than life size can escape the use of simplification and symbol, or avoid some kind of point of view; and the details that result can fix an edition absolutely in its period.

In the most widely used modern maps (the 1:50,000 series) the outstanding example of highlighting is the roads. In terms of position these are shown as accurately as they ever will be within the limits of surveying techniques. But their width is out of all proportion to their real size. Even minor roads are drawn at a scale that would make them about 50 yards wide. This, of course, is a reflection not just of the geographical importance of modern roads, but the fact that this is where most of us use maps *from*.

Roads and tracks are a significantly well-drawn feature of the first edition OS, which is not so surprising when you consider the origins of the Ordnance Survey. It was set up in 1791 to provide the British Army with accurate maps of the south coast during a period when French invasion seemed imminent. Its early years coincided with a period of great social and economic upheaval. Agriculture was in a state of revolution, there was bitterness and uprising in the countryside and wholesale migrations to the expanding cities, and the authorities clearly thought it was in their interest to have a clear picture of these unstable territories.

Given their social and political roles, these maps had to be as topically accurate as was practicable. You can consequently learn a good deal about the detailed changes in the landscape by comparing them with modern maps, or with the modern landscape itself. You will, of course, see a great number of roads and buildings that were not there at the beginning of the last century, and even, perhaps, a number of timber plantations. But in the countryside the story has largely been one of loss, and you're more likely to notice what has gone – a demolished farmstead or a drained fen. Long-established features like this often leave some persistent trace in the landscape long after they have vanished, and amongst the most exciting discoveries to be made with old maps is unravelling the origins of these remains. A narrow pool near a stream, for instance, may turn out to be a vanished mill-leat, or the hammer pond of a seventeenth-century furnace. A huge, reversed bank-and-ditch may be the boundary of a medieval deer park.

These remnants have become known as landscape 'ghosts', which nicely suggests the previous existence of something more substantial as well as a mysterious modern presence. In my own parish the best ghosts are botanical – some clumps of wood anemone that survive, stubbornly and quite untypically, along unploughed edges of an arable field and in some grassy road islands nearby. I'd always been mystified by their origins until I saw (on the first-edition OS) that they were growing on the site of a wood that had been cleared over fifty years ago.

The 'Tyes' that Edward Thomas rhapsodized over in East Anglia are also a kind of ghost or residue of small, self-contained settlements on what was once commonland. Typically they are a cluster of houses at the junction of several roads with the tapering, fan-like pattern that tracks form on un-fenced land. On the first OS maps you can often see the 'green' that was the Tye's original 'home range'.

Geoffrey Grigson even managed to track down the kiln where the bricks for his Wiltshire house were made. The 1828 OS map showed kilns some 5 miles away, and on some hard, flat ground near the overgrown clay-pits he was able to find bricks which exactly matched those in his house.

The OS still regards itself as a contemporary service, and its paramount duty as the recording of *useful* information. And this, of course, ensures that future historians will find our maps as valuable as we find those of the last century. Maps are documentary evidence and of no value as historical records unless they accurately reflect the needs and attitudes of the period in which they were made.

To this end the OS works with several consultative committees, representing every kind of user, from casual walkers to government departments and nationalized industries. Their advice helps shape the current codes with which the cartographers work, which decree, for example, how a milestone should be differentiated from a milepost, and which post offices merit having their letter boxes annotated with 'LB'. The consultative committees have recently recommended that the new edition of the 1:50,000 series should carry again those tiny representational trees which show whether a wood is broad-leaved or coniferous. These were taken out to reduce clutter a few years ago, but users have pleaded successfully for them to be put back.

The Ordnance Survey is also guided by the importance of usefulness when it comes to the vexed question of 'correct' place names. Although there are occasional requests that maps should use traditional (which often means archaic) names for places and features, the OS insists that a map's duty is to record common usage. If there is a dispute it normally accepts the word of the landowner or tenant, as the person most likely to determine the currency. But the owner must sign a form (and these are available for public scrutiny) to testify that the name originates with him or her. Although the OS retains the right to have the last word, it makes determined efforts to keep to this policy. There is a story that some of the obscure Gaelic place names in the far north of Scotland, diligently obtained from local citizens and inscribed on the map, are rather less than decent in translation!

True or not, I find this a cheering tribute to the Ordnance Survey's strongly democratic character. Their surveyors aren't alone amongst public servants in having the authority to go where they wish on private land, but they are unusual in using the information they gather for such a public document, which is increasingly a work of art and history as well as geography. I like to think that OS maps reflect the belief that at a fundamental level the surface of the land is a common heritage. Every one of us has the right to consult the National Map, and every one of us, in some small way, is featured on it.

Damp Humours

First published in *The Countryman*, 1974

Otmoor is an area of rough, wet pastureland just east of Oxford and has a small claim to fame in that its chequered network of dykes is believed to have given Lewis Carroll the idea for the chessboard scene in *Alice Through the Looking Glass*. I must admit that my first glimpse of this boggy plain suggested something much less orderly – a semi-wasteland, ragged and unfinished.

I was in rural conference with some publishing colleagues at the time – an indulgence we allowed ourselves every summer. We always called it our 'retreat'; but this was the first time our hotel had actually once been a priory. Out on the edge of this lonely moor, embattled with ancient trees and walled gardens, it seemed an ideal spot for a spell of the contemplative life.

But it was mid-June, and blazing hot. Even when we were forced out into the garden, the spotted flycatchers flicking about our tables were just as tantalizingly soporific as the lime-shaded lawn had looked through the lounge window. What a way to spend a summer afternoon!

After dinner, in the spare hour we had before the late-night session began, I'd had enough, and trudged off to these 4 square miles of marshland which looked so invitingly odd on the map, stuck there in the shires.

I couldn't have picked a better time for my first visit to Otmoor. The dusk made its outlines obscure and slightly sinister. The fields, such as I could see of them in the gloom, bristled with sedges and rushes. There were tufts of bramble and osier, rattling with the interminable reelings of grasshopper warblers. The trees were short and sparse, a few craggy willows and decaying elms in scattered belts along the field edges. Bulky and hunched silhouettes that they were in

51

this failing light, they seemed on the point of collapsing under their own weight into the ground. One, close to me, actually had, and on it a little owl was bobbing, eyes glaring into the tussocks. Minutes before I had to dash back for that last session he flew down into the grass for a kill.

I walked out on to the moor every early morning for the rest of our stay, along hedges that were brimming with singing blackcaps and garden warblers. Once I heard a few bars from a nightingale. And I came to grips with Otmoor's basic humour: its immutable, inescapable wetness. I went into breakfast every morning drenched to the knees.

Otmoor did not seem as brooding on those early-morning walks as it had during that first twilight visit; nor has it on the occasions I have been back since. There is only a hint now of the forbidding presence the 'great swamp' must have possessed when they rang a bell every winter's evening from the tower of St Mary's in Charlton to guide benighted travellers across the waste. Many of the fenny fields have been enclosed and drained, and the duck which used to haunt the floodwater in thousands during the winter are now more often counted in dozens. In some ways Otmoor is now no more than a distillation of the surrounding landscape, an Oxfordshire pasture taken to its limits. The dykes are deeper, the willows more stunted, the grass coarser, the horizon more uncompromisingly flat.

Yet the 'damp vapours' which the inhabitants used to blame for their continuous debility aren't that easily exorcized. Otmoor lies in a bowl formed by 450 feet of impenetrable clay, and the water is ineradicable, turning every untended corner and undredged dyke into a lush tangle of rushes and teasel. Leland, visiting the site of yet another Otmoor priory (the medieval Abbey of Oddington, which the rheumatic monks vacated after a few months), described it as 'more fitted for an ark than a monastery'.

And Otmoor's 'seven towns' still circle the moor warily, like shoreline villages on an inland sea. They seem to face away from the waste. Walk 100 yards down any of the tracks that lead from them into the moor and they have vanished from sight.

That any of Otmoor's character survives is the result of the doggedness of its inhabitants, who for centuries have been battling against absentee landowners, road builders, and water companies, who have all cast covetous eyes on its rich and empty acres. In the eleventh century Otmoor was the common pasture of all the surrounding villages, and many cottagers made quite adequate incomes by putting out geese. The old winding dykes and tracks lined with pollard willows that are now all that remains of the moor in many parts, were set down by these anonymous commoners. But in the early nineteenth century one of the largest landlords, the Duke of Marlborough, successfully petitioned for a Parliamentary Enclosure Award for almost the entire moor, including schemes for extensive drainage and fencing. It was one of the most unjust enactments of this sorry episode in English agricultural history, and the cottagers and smaller commoners found either that they could not establish their ancient rights by law and so received no allotments in compensation, or, having received an allotment, could not meet the enormous legal and fencing costs.

In September 1829 there was a mass uprising against the enclosure. More than a thousand people marched round the 7-mile boundary of the moor, tearing down all the fences. The Yeomanry arrived and the Riot Act was read, but the commoners refused to disperse. Forty-four of them were arrested and sent off to Oxford jail. In Oxford it happened to be the day of the St Giles Fair, and there a great crowd attacked the troops and rescued the prisoners. Back on the moor itself, the cattle were turned out to graze in common again.

But though the commoners fought on, both in law and in the fields, for another decade, the Enclosure was eventually imposed by force. And ironically, to round off this sad story of armed occupation, Otmoor has recently been used as a bombing range, 'a marked advance', as W. G. Hoskins observed, 'over the simple common grazing of the Dark Ages'.

I last visited Otmoor with a friend one gloomy February morning. We saw more cattle than birds, but the old swamp was lurking behind the electric fence. It trapped our car as we were parking, a small levy for two centuries of abuse. As

53

Landscapes

my friend remarked as she shook yet another ball of sodden
clay off her boots, it did put new meaning into the phrase
'bound to the soil'.

The Tides of March

First published in *Good Housekeeping*, April 1982

I first read about the tidal woods on the Fal estuary in *A Nature Conservation Review*,* a weighty compendium of the 'biological sites of national importance to nature conservation in Britain' not given to travel agents' flights of fancy. But I sensed a rather special excitement in its restrained account of strange natural ceremonials under the Cornish full moon: 'The site is a complex of saltings, salt marsh, carr and . . . fine natural transition to alder–willow woodland still tidal at the equinoxes, a habitat type now almost extinct in Europe . . . 120 species of flowering plants and ferns, many not normally associated with the inter-tidal zone . . . . Mature oak trees survive occasional flooding with water showing as much as one-tenth sea water salinity.'

A high tide in springtime wood: it sounded faintly preposterous, like a cornfield on a mountain top. But then we will persist in glamorizing the spring. Against all experience we forget that it's as much a time for a great rearranging of the hemisphere's air and water as it is the season for breaking buds. In Cornwall, especially, spring can be tumultuous. It brings gales which race capriciously up the peninsula from the south-west, hard on the tails of incoming eels and swallows who have crossed whole oceans in the hope of a quiet summer here. Walter White, who walked from London to Land's End in 1854, found the wind all but took over his senses. The gales, he marvelled, 'carried the salt spray ten miles inland, so that it may be tasted on window-panes, and the blades of corn.'

Seven thousand years ago, when most of lowland England was cloaked in trees, sea-lashed woods must have been much commoner. But they would have been urgent, fleeting places.

* Ed. D. A. Ratcliffe, Cambridge University Press, 1977.

Trees don't take kindly to provinces of hurtling gales and shifting sands. Little clumps would have 'got away' here and there on the highest level of dunes, in pockets of earth caught in cliff faces, or on the more stable banks of silted estuaries; thickets of willow, blackthorn, oak, taking their chances for ten, maybe fifty years. Then there would be a run of winter floods, or a landslip, and the shoreline would be scoured clean again. Today they do not even have these brief chances. If a patch of ground is secure enough to grow trees, even temporarily, it will be worth someone's while to commandeer it for crops or villas.

Yet you can wind your way inland through the jumble of creeks that fray the edges of the river between Feock and Truro, and every one is fringed with glistening silt right up to the trees. You have to travel north-east along the route of the Fal for 10 miles from the estuary mouth before the river is narrow enough to be crossed by a stone bridge. If you look upstream here, between the steeply wooded sides of the valley, you can believe for a moment that you are on an ordinary West Country river. But something is not quite right. Either the woods are too steep or the flood-plain between them too flat. They meet in an unnaturally sharp boundary, and along it there is white encrustation on the lower branches of the oaks. Is it lichen, or salt? Follow its line and you can see how the dip between the tilted oakwoods is being steadily taken over by young willows and alders. You have the uneasy feeling that you are too low down, or that the smooth sward of marshland grasses is deceptively, and probably dangerously, high.

If you turn round and face towards the sea, there still isn't much comfort in the prospect. The river broadens out more quickly than the woods and they meet sharply half a mile away. You are in the mouth of a natural bottle that is filling with water. In front of the incoming tide curlews and shelduck are taking flight. You cannot see them, but their lilting calls seem to be coming from the woods, as if these marshland birds had taken to the trees. Do they know something you don't?

I should mention one more thing. The water that trickles thinly out of the woods, broadens into a surge beneath the bridge, then begins to spread like a stain across the estuarine grasses, is the colour of clotted cream.

The mould for this bizarre landscape was set even before the Ice Ages began. That would have been a satisfying time to have been a Cornishperson, with the rest of southern England still languishing under the sea, and forests of wild rhododendron and magnolia growing on the site of modern shrubberies. Between them flowed the fledgling rivers Fal and Helford, well-behaved freshwater streams then, presumably, with quiet banks of reed and water-mint.

Then, about two million years ago, the southern coast of Cornwall subsided, and its river estuaries drowned in the sea. They have been tidal ever since, and woods have had little chance of forming below the highwater mark. Except, that is, on the Fal. This labyrinthine natural drain, gathering most of its water from heavy rains washing through the china-clay beds below Bodmin, and having to funnel through steep-sided valleys on its way to the sea, has swung between flooding and silting as far back as the Middle Ages. But by the beginning of the nineteenth century the silt was certainly winning, and the woods were on the march across the flood-plain. The willows that still flourish there used to be cut to make local crab and lobster pots.

In the middle of the nineteenth century silting was speeded up still further by the china-clay works at St Austell, which were discharging enough sediment to colour the Fal and most of its tributaries white. It is a rich sediment, and since 1878 the valley wood has been able to extend nearly 3 miles from Tregony to the bridge at Ruan Lanihorne. This is the most truly tidal of the local woods. But every creek and low-lying corner has some trace of this ancient mix of trees and sea. West of Ruan the road corkscrews up through Lamorran Wood, fording a point where brackish water seeps over and under the tarmac. The sea itself lies just 100 yards into the wood, lapping a bank of Cornish elms and primroses. Then, just past Lamorran, it fills a creek that runs parallel with the road, and changes in colour from kaolin white to livid Amazonian green as you move further inland.

From here on the lanes bury themselves deeper in the

woods. You glimpse flashes of yellow behind dry-stone walls, where cultivated daffodils are growing in field patterns scarcely changed since Celtic times. Scarlet-flowered tree rhododendrons, escaped from isolated country houses' gardens, light up the leafless woods as they may have done a million years ago.

You cannot reach every stretch of estuarine wood. At St Michael Penkevil the road ended with great finality at a church on an intricately walled mound, and with every exit from the hamlet blocked by estate gates. Beyond one of them, so my map said, lay another landscape curiosity: an estuarine deer park. I imagined the animals gazing at the white water like creatures in a Watteau painting. At Philleigh the paths down to Borlase and Pelgerran woods were much too muddy to tramp. Both water and sap, it seemed, were rising. In the village a well-outfitted, white-haired tramp strode out east for summer quarters. A barn owl floated across the lane behind him. And in the churchyard of St Filii de Eglosros they were giving the grass and wild garlic its first mow of the year.

So the next afternoon, the first of spring, I went to the most truly tidal wood, sat on a badger track and waited for the equinoctial high water. There was a cold wind out in the open marsh, but in amongst the twisted oak coppice and heather it was warm and still. In summer I imagine it could be quite stifling. Buzzards floated above the wood, and as the tide began to turn, invisible curlews piped overhead. When it came, the high tide was not quite the dramatic mix of wood and water that I had hoped for. It lapped milkily and rather sedately round the gold saxifrage and yellow flag, but never seemed to *flood* the wood.

But that night I was woken by rain and spray lashing my sea-front hotel. A south-westerly gale had blown up and was driving the tide over St Mawes quay. The highest waves were spraying the second-storey windows. Down at Ruan, it had been a night of devastation. A film of white clay lay over the whole of the valley, and the sea had even reached the lower levels of the oak wood. A windblown tidemark of twine and polystyrene flotsam lay tangled up with the lowest primroses. I had read of another surprise flood-tide in October 1963. The animal inhabitants of the valley had had to improvise a mass escape, with spiders and beetles climbing to the tops of tall plants, bugs hopping across the surface of the water, and voles (pursued by flocks of predatory gulls) swimming for their lives. I thought of them that night fleeing on rafts of detergent bottles. It would have been funny if it was not so tragic.

It rained mercilessly on the drive back, until the sun came out over the Thames at Henley on a meeker kind of spring. Cornwall, as they say, is still a foreign country.

The Yorkshire Dales

First published as 'Up hill and down dale' in *In Britain*, April 1983

It was meant to have been one of those relaxing midweek breaks, a couple of days in the Dales, an ambling holiday. We had picked the moment with what we thought was connoisseurs' precision – late June, when the Wharfe trout would be in season and the wild roses flowering over the dry-stone walls. We were even prepared, after a fashion, for the repeated and dispiriting downpours of one of the wettest Junes on record. No, it wasn't weather or wrongfooting that turned our leisurely strolling into a forced march, but my longing to see a bird's-eye primrose, which reached such unreasonable and unassuageable proportions that we covered almost the whole of Wharfedale in forty-eight hours flat.

For those unfamiliar with this little floral siren I should explain that it is, by common consent, amongst the half-dozen most exquisite of all our native flowers. It is like an alpine in habit, with a posy of coral pink flowers – each with a pure yellow eye – carried a few inches above a rosette of dusty, grey-green leaves. That great champion of the rock garden, Reginald Farrer, who spent his life collecting alpines in the most exotic mountains of the world, still loved this modest primula of his native West Riding above all others. The Yorkshire Dales are its heartland, and there are those of a romantic disposition who think it should replace that alien white rose from the Middle East as the county flower.

But all this is hearsay. I have only seen bird's-eyes once, and that was in Cumbria, in tantalizingly small numbers.

Still, the chance of seeing meadows powdered pink was only one amongst a number of pleasant prospects as we set off from Threshfield, down the hill to the wide bridge at Grassington, and headed upstream along the east bank of the Wharfe. It was only a matter of minutes since we had disembarked from the long drive up the M1, and we were happy just to be unencumbered at last. Towards us straggled lines of dejected schoolchildren, cocooned in day-glo anoraks and big boots from which they seemed to have abandoned all hope of ever hatching.

Things soon began to perk up. About half a mile from Grassington the first crops of limestone burst through the stolid valley clays, and the oily swirlings of a southern river give way to the dash and noise of an upland stream. It is astonishing, the quickening that limestone brings to a landscape. You would think it was generating ozone. The colours are sharper, the air more exhilarating, even the birds more hectic. Within a few minutes we had seen a dipper, with pebble-white breast and whirring wings, darting between boulders that had been worn flat by countless winter floods. A sandpiper bobbed at the water's edge. And further up the bank the cracks in the rocks were filled with flowers whose colours looked quite piercing against the pale stone: veins of purple thyme running down into the river, tufts of yellow rock-rose and magenta cranesbills.

For a while we passed through open woodland which climbed in shallow terraces up the sides of the valley. Then the footpath veered away from the river and led us on to the back-road to Conistone, and face to face with yet another group of forlorn hikers. 'How many miles to Grassington?' begged their teacher. Only a couple, we replied, thinking to encourage them. Disbelief was followed by despair, even after we had charitably halved the distance. They limped off for the longest mile of their life, and we strode on to Conistone with weariness not even the remotest worry.

Pride before a fell! We should have known better, but the lane had a beguiling cosiness. Raspberries and wild geraniums draped the verges, as if they were long cottage gardens. Traffic was part of another world, a silent procession on the far side of the river, where the main road was tucked under the looming face of Kilnsey Crag. This was a walker's lane, and we were in possession. We meandered on, chatting in a somewhat mandarin way about the collective word for the herons we had seen loping along the river (is it a siege?), about how well chilled

Burgundy would go with wild raspberries, and nibbling the aniseed-flavoured seeds from sweet cicely plants to stave off hunger pangs.

It took the curlews to put a stop to all this precious nonsense and remind us where we were. They came flying down from the hayfields to circle over our heads, their skirling calls echoing back from the high rocks. We left the road and followed them, up the slow incline towards Conistone Old Pasture.

The slope itself was gentle enough. It was the walls that were the trouble. They were close on 6 feet tall in places and unnervingly narrow. Even the stepping stones that had been set in them seemed more like arrowheads than footholds. And no sooner had we finished the tremulous climb over one wall than another loomed up ahead. The whole fellside up to nearly 1,000 feet was a labyrinth of compartments smaller and more effectively enclosed than I had ever seen at such an altitude.

As it turned out, we were clambering over a piece of Wharfedale history, preserved in stone. Up until the close of the eighteenth century the Old Pasture had been one of the largest of Conistone's common grazing lands. It was stocked chiefly with cattle and managed according to an intricate system of bylaws designed to reconcile the rights of individual graziers with the need to prevent overgrazing. The whole arrangement was deeply rooted in the ancient village economy, and the rights to a certain proportion of the 'beast gates' (one beast gate was feeding and grazing for one 'made beast', or full-grown animal) went with the holdings of each tenement or cottage. The problem was that beast gates were inherited, and repeatedly divided up and sold, so that it became all but impossible to translate an individual's rights into a number of animals. By the eighteenth century overgrazing had become a threat to everyone's livelihood. So Conistone applied to Parliament for an Act of Enclosure (a rare instance of willing and voluntary enclosure). This was awarded in 1801, and the inhabitants set about dividing up the Old Pasture into enclosures whose respective sizes reflected the graziers' portions of the overall beast gate. The walls they built still remain, and I imagine they are as high as they are because they once had to keep in horses and oxen as well as sheep.

We were tickled by the idea of 'beast gates'. The phrase made it sound as if cattle were as unpredictable in numbers as football crowds, or as if just getting into (or out of) this fortified pasture was the chief measure of one's beasthood. I can't deny we felt a twinge of existential relief as we made it over the last wall and into the open grassland on the hilltop.

Up here it is a landscape pared down to the bone. Limestone sills stretch out along the contour lines. Limestone rocks are strewn about between them where the raw materials for the walls were hacked out. Limestone 'pavements', broken up into great slabs by ancient glaciers and centuries of rainfall, shelter woodland plants in their deep fissures. We followed the sweep of the terraces back in the direction of Grassington, through sheets of rock-roses so dense that their pollen scented the wind.

The great gorge of Dib Beck and the precipitous slopes of Grass and Bastow Woods that hung on its edge were too steep to venture in, but we could see that they were studded with prodigious flowers: orpine, meadow-rue, marjoram and yet more species of cranesbill. We were in some kind of botanical paradise, and it was with a shameful lack of gratitude that it was just at this moment, just as we were making our way through the hazel scrub, with magenta geraniums and mountain pansies all around our feet, that we began to miss the bird's-eye. Hadn't no less a florophile than Geoffrey Grigson described their flowers in May and June, decorating 'every bank, every slope, every corner between the grey outcrop of limestone'? Why not our banks and slopes?

But they would have to wait till the next day. We had been walking solidly for more than four hours, and the hotel menu was becoming more than just a passing fantasy. We found our way back into the village along the most comforting of green lanes, that had probably taken men and animals off the fells at the end of the day for a thousand years.

*   *   *

The next day broke with a cold, damp mist hanging low over the hills. We needed something to stiffen our resolve, so, fired by the enthusiasm of another fine writer on flowers, Robert Gathorne-Hardy, who had seen 'great glimmering pools of lilac, filling damp places in the pastures' not half a dozen miles from Threshfield, we set off on our treasure hunt at a pace that defied both common sense and good taste. But, goodness, it did give us a flavour of the place.

I can recommend Malham Moor in a good wet fog. It was just the setting for the melancholy piping of curlews and the cackle of the invisible gulls that were nesting in colonies around the peaty tarns. Sheep and stones merged into a general humpiness in which the sheep, by and large, were the most static part. We knew how they felt. At 1,300 feet we could see no more than 20 yards, and though we tried to persuade ourselves that this continual spray of Yorkshire hard water was just the thing for the complexion, we could barely even face into the driving rain, let alone look for putative primroses. On the map there were miles of bogland between us and the delights (also invisible no doubt) of Malham itself, and we took fright, trudged back to the car and drove there instead, an eerie roller-coaster ride up and down through plates of mist. There were no bird's-eyes to be seen at Malham, but the Tarn was an extraordinary vision, merging with the fog into a single plane of frosted light. Somewhere in the middle a solitary fisherman floated between land and sky.

We stopped for elevenses in a lonely pub near Hawkswick Moor and watched the Old Trafford Test Match on a giant television. That too was plunging in and out of rain – *our* rain, I should add, before it was beefed up by the Pennines. But there seemed to be quite long gaps between their downpours, so we set off again, this time for the upper reaches of Wharfe-dale. Between Kettlewell and Buckden the river is lined with tiny, walled hay meadows, and the honey-coloured grasses, dappled with buttercups, mountain pansies, cranesbills and eyebrights were just ready for mowing. The same plants grew wild along the river bank, and these queer-shaped enclosures, too small to be cut by machine, had probably just been en-closed from the natural vegetation of the flood-plain. I thought of Andrew Marvell's cryptic and intense 'mowing' poems, written three hundred years ago whilst he was staying at Nun Appleton, on the far eastern reaches of the Wharfe. In 'The Mower against Gardens' he contrasts the rough harmony of haymaker and hay with the arrogant dominance of nature expressed in fashionable gardens:

> The Tulip, white, did for complexion seek;
>   And learn'd to interline its cheek:
> Its Onion root they then so high did hold,
>   That one was for a meadow sold

Obviously too cultivated by half ourselves, we failed to read the weather yet again, and had to walk back under the lee of Cam Pasture with our heads bowed against the rain. On the way we passed another Dales' speciality, the melancholy thistle, so called because of the sad droop of its solitary flowerhead, and we knew how *that* felt, too. How many miles to Grassington?

Later we glimpsed Langstrothdale and Skoska Wood and Ghaistrill's Strid. We saw Ings and Garths and a farming landscape still echoing with ancient Norse. At Litton we sat by the Crystal Beck and forded the Skirfare, in full spate from the rains. Along the bank the bushes were covered with water-weed from the previous night's flooding. In Heselden we tramped along gentle terraced grassland that was for all the world like a Cotswold combe. We kept to the well-marked and stiled footpaths here, making a mental note of suitably dry barns on the route, and not for the first time gave thanks for how generously this country had accommodated walkers. It is a tradition going back to the middle of the nineteenth century, when the railways first opened up the Dales to tourists. On this occasion it was the locals not the visitors who took up the battle to keep the footpaths open, and notably the Grassington botanist, herbal vet and radical rambler, John Crowther. Thirty years before the Kinder Scout Mass Trespass he was leading parties of Grassington residents to reopen walled-up stiles and destroy illicit 'Keep Out' notices. Later in his life he had an unknown orchid from Grass Wood named after him.

It was exactly at the moment that we decided to give up the search for our own (now unmentionable) rarity and relax, that the sun shone and we could see the entire length of a dale for the first time. The limestone, as is its way, took on the tones of sunlight, and the air was so clear that we could see a black rabbit standing like a felt cut-out in a distant meadow. We could also see what we had been half-glimpsing for the last two days, that behind all their differences there is unity about the Dales landscapes, a special kind of rightness. Everything is just where it should be: the walls, the trackways, the hay meadows in the rich valleys, the rough common grazing on the tops. Two thousand years of settlement have respected this natural order, and even today the Dales are still remarkably free of conifer plantations and forced arable fields. For that insight alone the madcap hike was worth it.

Back home, expert friends told us that we were *weeks* too late for the bird's-eyes. But we will get them next year,* in early June, with the help of a copy of Crowther's 1920 guidebook *Rambles round Grassington* if necessary. And if we still have no luck in Wharfedale there is always the magic country round Ribblesdale to explore, where the cracks in the limestone pavements are 8 feet deep, and where there is a wood full of waist-high geraniums that you can only enter by wading up a river.

* We did, in millions round the foothills of Ingleborough.

The New Forest

First published in *Vole*, July 1979, as a review of *The New Forest: 900 Years After* by Peter Tate, Macdonalds

This year the New Forest celebrates what is believed to be its 900th birthday. I have to put it like that as no one is sure when William the Conqueror annexed this considerable tract of southern England as a hunting estate. More than 500 square miles of woodland, heath and bog may have been involved, yet not a single document exists concerning the exact date or extent of afforestation. It's mentioned in Domesday, so presumably was well established by 1086; but the entry (*in Nova Foresta et circa eam*) is notorious for its complexity and ambiguity, and it still leaves great doubts about where, precisely, the forest boundaries were, which villages were put under forest law, and what restrictions these laws put upon agriculture. This much later it is possible to be rather more certain about a few matters – for instance, that the Forest has shrunk to 145 square miles, 105 of which are in 'public' or Crown ownership. But beyond that the old familiar muddles begin to appear. The geology of south-west Hampshire and the tenacity of its inhabitants have repeatedly confounded the ambitions of planners, land-grabbers, despots, agricultural improvers, tidiers, enclosers and developers of every complexion. As a result, the New Forest remains as a testament to the virtues and viability of the common use of land and as almost the only remaining stretch of lowland Britain where there is still the illusion of an ancient wilderness. It is also a unique remnant of Norman England, and if William – whose first monumental act of appropriation ironically helped make all later attempts unsuccessful – were to return, he would probably be able to find his way about without much difficulty.

My first encounter with the New Forest was on a camping holiday when I was about 15. It seemed to me then an awesome and hostile place, pitted with bogs, blanketed with scorching airs, wet and hot in ways that had more to do with imagined jungles than old England. Later, when I became more familiar with it, I began to appreciate its extraordinary variety of textures, and how these were reflections of the way the Forest had been seen and used by others. I remember seeing my first red deer here and, one autumn, the herds of pigs that are let out to forage when there is a good acorn crop, in the exercise of a right that still has only the old Norman word 'pannage' to describe it. I doubt if there is another place in England where the King's beasts and the commoners' still run together in the woods. It is midsummer dusks that I relish the most: the bog myrtle that spices the air in every damp valley, and the sweeter scent of lesser butterfly orchids on the grassy plains by Set Thorns; and the hot evenings when nightjars loll about on the dusty tracks through the heather, flitting always just a few yards ahead of you. Sometimes, if it is early enough in the summer, you may glimpse their breathtaking courtship displays, in which they skim and float over the surface of the heather, clapping their wings above their backs.

And at all times and seasons, there is that sense of a quiet tension between the wood and the heath: the stands of great beeches, now nearing their maturity, and the new, self-sown thickets of holly, birch and oak springing up on the heaths; yet the ponies and cattle staking their territory too, eating the woods back. In valleys like those near Berry Wood and Matley Bog the scene is uncannily like Maurice Wilson's reconstructions of Stone Age landscapes; only the animals have changed.

These are very partial images of the New Forest, the view of a casual visitor. It is easy to forget that as well as being a national treasure, it is also the working, common pasture of hundreds of local smallholders. Peter Tate is a local (though not a grazier) and his pleasantly discursive book *The New Forest: 900 Years After* covers many less usual, more parochial aspects. He is especially good on the Forest's tough little ponies, which are easy to look on as nothing more than attractive ornaments or schoolgirls' playthings, rather than as vital components of the whole Forest eco-system. They have been here since 1208 and play a fundamental role in keeping the heaths and plains open. It is sad to read of the numbers being shipped for their meat to Belgium (where their unborn foals are regarded as a delicacy) and that they and the Forest alike may be suffering from overstocking. I can forgive Peter Tate many of his rather breathless journalistic excesses for the sake of his pleas for what he calls the Forest's 'little lawn-mowers'.

The ponies appear many times in the book. They stray on to the village cricket pitches, and PSP (ponies stopped play) is a recognized abbreviation in Forest scorebooks. They used to mingle, and no doubt breed, with the gypsies' horses, when the New Forest was the stronghold of the 'lost tribe' and a Romany was respected as a kind of honorary commoner. The best-known chronicler of local gypsy life (and probably half Romany herself) was Juliette de Bairacli Levy, who had her own unique vision of the Forest. Peter Tate quotes her description of a bizarre swim in a flooded pond: 'The entire base . . . being grass, it is possible, when the rains have given the water sufficient depth, to swim there slowly and gaze down upon flowers like mer-things shining at the bottom.'

There are so many New Forests, so many harvests taken from them. There are arboreta, working gravel pits, golf courses and a model-aircraft flying area. It is the intricate system of mutual checks and balances between the multitude of different users of the Forest that has helped it survive against all the odds. For nine centuries the resolute (some would say stubborn) defence of their rights by all interested parties – and, indeed, by the soil itself, which is reckoned to be almost the poorest in Europe – has prevented any single faction gaining absolute control. Various kings tried to enclose the open heath and establish timber plantations, but were repeatedly blocked by the commoners, who succeeded in keeping the bulk of their grazing land open. Today it is the commoners who wish to improve the productivity of the heaths (especially the undrained boggy ones) and who are being restrained by conservationists who have the interest of marsh gentians and smooth snakes at heart. Nobody is completely satisfied, but then no one is ignored either.

The worst threat the Forest has ever faced resulted, typically, in an even stronger network of safeguards. In the late

1960s the Forestry Commission, which had become the Crown's executors in the Forest in 1923, drew up a plan for 'phasing out' the broadleaf trees of the 'Ancient and Ornamental Woodlands' and replacing them with quick-growing conifers. In 1970, after a nerveless piece of espionage, a group of local environmentalists exposed the Commission's plan. There was a national outcry, which led the Minister of Agriculture to draw up a mandate whose major objectives were that: 'The New Forest is to be regarded as a national heritage and priority given to the conservation of its traditional character . . . The Ancient and Ornamental Woodlands are to be conserved without regard to timber production objectives.' The affair played an important role in the revision of Forestry Commission policy nationally, and led to a new strategy for controlling tourist use of the Forest. It was a typical piece of Forest balancing, a way of safeguarding the 'national heritage' at the same time as reminding the nation that people and animals had a job of work to do here.

The long evolution of the New Forest has never had the orderliness and sense of direction beloved by modern planners. It has been quarrelsome, compromised and laboriously slow. In fact, the jostling for position and 'demonstration of presence' by New Foresters is like nothing so much as the way animals sort out their territorial claims over a stretch of land – which is perhaps the most appropriate style for the custodians of such an anciently wild habitat. In the future more conventional, so-called 'rational' planning is probably inevitable, given the increasing pressures on the Forest. But the authorities would do well to remember that it was not planning but a kind of organic evolution that was responsible for the Forest's variety, and probably the chief reason why it has survived. For it is, when you think about it, a complete anomaly: besieged by Southampton's expanding petrochemical complexes to the east, by Bournemouth's ribbon development to the south, by the Ministry of Defence to the north-west, it remains the largest and most luxuriant semi-natural landscape in north-western Europe. Despite the dubious airs surrounding it, its trees carry a collection of lichens (exceptionally sensitive to atmospheric pollution) unrivalled in southern Britain. It has demonstrated that even under conditions of quite intense grazing, native woodlands will regenerate, provided they have enough room; and that when there is room, it is possible to combine public access with the experience of solitude. Millions of people visit the Forest every year, yet it's still possible to walk for a whole day and not see another soul.

Many small faults could be found with the management of the Forest, and its future immunity from oil or mineral extraction is by no means secure. But for the moment it remains perhaps the finest working example of an alternative route to efficient resource use, where diversity rather than size of output is the goal. It might, of course, be possible to drench the whole area with fertilizers, clear the trees and plant out carrots. (Indeed, one of the first agribusinessmen, Arthur Young, wanted to do just that.) But it would be a costly and wasteful fate for a stretch of land that grows so many other things with scarcely any input at all. It may be hard to put a price on the multitude of products of the Forest cooperative, but they make an impressive list: 18,000 acres of timber, and nearly 10,000 more of superb ancient trees; 5,000 head of stock; 1,000,000 'camper-nights' a year; cicadas, wild gladioli, free-range pigs, a gypsy floating in a pond. . . .

After the Elm

First published in *Vole*, February 1980

There are two decisive moments in the prehistory of our landscape: the opening-up of the Channel in 5500 BC, which turned Britain into an island, and what is known as the Elm Decline two thousand years later, during which the first evidence of settled agriculture begins to show up. Both events are momentous examples of the natural and human forces that together create landscapes. But it's the second that always fires the imagination more – the long march of those small-framed Mediterranean farmers, crossing the new sea with their domestic animals and pots of cereal seeds, hacking out their little smallholdings in the wildwood, and leaving behind them, preserved in peat, pollen remains of the weeds that have dogged agriculturalists ever since. And it is such a poignant phrase, the Decline – suggestive of the Fall, the passing of the Tree, the end of Eden . . . . You have to pull yourself up sharply to remember that it is an exact botanical description, not an epithet by an early Creationist. Although these neolithic settlers were clearing the forest more extensively and more permanently than ever before, the 'Elm Decline' does not strictly refer to a reduction in elm *trees* (about which we can know very little), but to a dramatic fall in the proportion of elm *pollen* in contemporary peat deposits, to about half its former frequency. The reasons for this are still not fully understood. But there is archaeological evidence that elm was highly valued as a fodder plant, and that its leafy branches were cut and fed to stalled cattle. This would have prevented the cut trees flowering, and led to a decline in the overall elm pollen. It also amounted to an early form of management, and the trees which were lopped should have lived long and productive lives as a result.

But they appear not to have done, and pollarding for fodder

can't be the only reason for the Decline. Dr Oliver Rackham has calculated that there were some ten million acres of elm in Britain at the time, and for half of these to have had their pollen production stopped would have entailed half a million adults spending the entire spring and summer pollarding elms, and a total population ten-fold larger than existed at this period. He suggests instead that the Decline may have resulted from an early wave of Dutch elm disease, following (as such infectious plant diseases often do) the introduction of agriculture to a previously wild habitat, and the subsequent moving about of people and wood. Moreover 'the ground occupied by the dead elms would have been used as grassland or arable. Such a process, with civilization helping the spread of the disease, and the disease helping the spread of civilization, could enable a much smaller population to go through most of the elms in NW Europe in a few centuries or even decades.'*

I've digressed at some length about this early landscape riddle, as such complex accommodations between man and the wild don't really fit our current view of the world, in which things are presumed to be either natural or man-made (and we seem certain there is a difference). Brian Clouston's and Kathy Stansfield's collection of essays† on the course and implication of our current Elm Decline is no exception, and they base their argument on a vision of the countryside as a man-made construction in which the basic components just happen to be living. We must be grateful to all concerned for making this clear at the outset, where they also declare their credentials. Five out of the eight contributors are (or have been) landscape architects, and though their hearts are clearly in the right place, I fear their heads have been turned by their professional calling.

It would be churlish to find nothing but fault with a book whose authors are so evidently devoted to the value and delights of trees, and it is only because their perspective causes them to perpetuate one of the most persistent and damaging myths about the origins of our countryside that I feel it is

---

* *Ancient Woodland*, Edward Arnold, 1980.
† *After the Elm*, Heinemann, 1979.

important to do so. At the heart of the book is a single thread of argument about nothing less than the nature of landscape, and in particular the 'classic' English landscape. Are landscapes artefacts or natural encrustations? Do they come about by accident or, literally, by design? These are currently questions of the greatest importance, since we're aware that our rural landscape is changing dramatically (the loss of the elms being both a real feature and a symbol of this change), and are trying to decide whether to 'do' anything about it. Both the extreme views of landscape creation described above imply drastic responses, either of tolerant inaction, or radical replanning.

The authors' position is clear, and the syllogism on which their case rests is this: the classic English landscape was a product of deliberate rural planning during the Parliamentary Enclosures in the late eighteenth and early nineteenth centuries. This landscape is now senescent and economically irrelevant. We therefore need similarly deliberate planning (guided by landscape architects) if we are to create a comparable twentieth-century landscape.

This belief is clung to so tenaciously that it even distorts the factual evidence. Brian Clouston writes that 'Between 1761 and 1844 there were more than 2,500 Acts of Parliament dealing with over forty million acres [*sic*] of open fields.' The precise figures are 2,911 Acts covering four and a half million acres of open field and pasture.

Nor do the authors mention the additional 1,893 Acts relating to the enclosure of more than two million acres of commonland. They do not seem to understand that enclosure was not simply concerned with partitioning up the old open arable fields, but involved a total reorganization of the whole parish economy, including road straightening, drainage, woodland clearance and the ploughing up of heathland, and that probably as many 'wild' trees were destroyed in the process as were planted in the new hedges.

In the final chapter, 'Towards a New Landscape', Carter Cobham and Lloyd compare the classic farming landscape with the formal landscaped garden: 'The English landscape style created in the eighteenth century . . . informal, apparently almost casual . . . the result of the English style was almost to merge the landowner's park with his farmland, the general fabric of the countryside.' The suggestion here is that the farm landscape was modelled on that of the park, whereas in most cases what happened was the exact reverse. Many of Capability Brown's large-scale 'landskips' (for example, Heveningham, Woodstock and Beechwood) were made largely by the simple expedient of enclosing (and destroying any inconsiderately placed farms and hamlets) existing areas of long-mature farmland.

It is astonishing that despite the work of popularizers like W. G. Hoskins, this belief that the English rural landscape was created *de novo* in the last two hundred years should still persist. It is seventy years since E. C. K. Gonner's classic *Common land and inclosure* showed that less than a fifth of England was enclosed during the era of Parliamentary Awards. His demonstration that the bulk of the English landscape was shaped much earlier and in much more informal ways has been supported by every historian who has taken the trouble to go back to the documents or go out in the field. Are we then talking at cross purposes about different kinds of 'classic' landscape? I do not think so. I think, for instance, we could all agree that Constable's paintings come close to catching what we understand to be this classic landscape. The authors certainly mention them – and the elms they so often feature – with approval.

The Suffolk countryside which Constable immortalized is one whose history is very well documented. We know, for example, that there were virtually no open fields in the area to be enclosed by the eighteenth century. There were only 115 parliamentary Acts for the whole of the county, and more than half of these were for commonland. Except for a couple of hundred acres near Finningham, the open field enclosures concerned the sandy sheepwalk country in the far west of the county. In the Stour Valley, Parliamentary Enclosure was concerned exclusively with the *destruction* of existing features. The one painting by Constable which specifically tackles an enclosure landscape is an oil sketch of East Bergholt Common under plough (Victoria & Albert Museum, No. 144). It is a bleak, virtually treeless prospect, painted in the spring of 1816, less than a year after the passing of the Act for the enclosure of the common. Archaeological and documentary evidence shows that the bulk of the claylands of central Suffolk were being enclosed as early as the tenth century, and that the process was more or less complete by the beginning of the fifteenth.

Constable's principle subjects, then, were plainly not eighteenth- or nineteenth-century Parliamentary Enclosure landscapes. But perhaps it is not the period that matters, but the *detail* of the 'classic' landscape. Again, we can describe this exactly from the paintings (or from a set of modern photographic postcards, for that matter). It is, above all, a small-scale, asymmetrical landscape, of small, irregularly shaped fields, old hedges, winding lanes, deep ditches, banks, moats, oddly shaped copses and old trees – including elms. It is a landscape instantly recognizable as the romantic stereotype of old England, and we know very well where to find it: in Devon, Dorset, Hereford, the Weald of Kent, Sussex, and south Norfolk, for example. Was the basic pattern of the landscape in these places (regardless of how it may have been altered subsequently) established by conscious planning in the 'age of improvement'? On the contrary, both documentary and surviving field evidence point to a continuous process of individual, piecemeal enclosure and landscape moulding, beginning in the Bronze Age.

If, working from the documents again, we search for landscapes that were created by something we would understand today as 'planning', we end up in a belt of Middle England that stretches from Wiltshire through central Oxfordshire and the Midlands up to south Yorkshire. The landscapes here are typified by symmetry and uniformity: precisely rectangular fields, low hawthorn hedges, straight roads. Two hundred years on they have acquired a character of their own, but it is blander, less suprising, less varied than what Oliver Rackham has called 'ancient countryside'.

There is a story that the winding lanes of East Anglia (where the country can be so flat that their bends and dog-legs are incomprehensible) got that way because the road builders liked to work with their backs to the wind, which was apt to blow 'every ole way'. It's only a joke, but it does catch something of the fundamental difference between the ways the two kinds of landscape were created. Ancient countryside *evolved*, out of centuries of do-it-yourself enterprise involving the whole community. Neolithic men laid out the first ridge-way tracks for the safe passage of their flocks. The Celts built up complex field systems where woodland had been cleared on light soils, and surrounded them with immense banks and boundary ditches, or stone walls built from glacial rubble. The Saxons cut out fields from the heavier forest on the wet clays, leaving (or planting) the first hedges between them. Medieval peasants beat out our present pattern of footpaths and lanes with feet and carts, began pollarding trees that are still alive today, and enclosed – on their own initiative and in their own style – more little corners of waste and wood than were ever parcelled up by the nineteenth-century bureaucrats. And in many parts of England remains of all these developments persist in the landscape, for each new development did not obliterate the previous one, but was woven into it.

By contrast, the landscapes of the eighteenth- and nineteenth-century improvers were planned – on a drawing board, as often as not – with little sensitivity towards the natural features of the land or for the people who lived and worked on it. One Enclosure landscape looks much like another, whether you are in Dorset or Leicestershire, and they mostly lack that human scale and quirkiness that can make ancient countryside so sympathetic. (Incidentally, the fact that many of the new Enclosure landscapes included hedges studded with thousands of genetically identically elms is one of the reasons Dutch elm disease was able to take such a hold, or at least such a *conspicuous* hold, in these areas.)

The breakdown of the grid-pattern of Parliamentary Enclosure, as a result of tree diseases and deliberate hedge clearance, has theoretically given us a chance to pick up the threads of landscape evolution where they were so tidily snipped off in the eighteenth century. But instead of this, the authors of *After the Elm* would have us follow the example of the Enclosure Commissioners and go through the whole unhappy bureaucratic imposition all over again. They talk repeatedly of the importance of a 'Grand Design', and are so convinced of the importance of their own jobs that the text reads at times like a publicity leaflet: 'The landscape professions served us uniquely well in the eighteenth century. It is time they were asked and expected to do so again. . . . It is therefore more important than ever that the initial plan is prepared by professional landscape designers and is strong, cohesive and convincing, not a mere collation of haphazard suggestions by many people.'

Given the consequences of *laissez-faire* policies in the modern countryside I suppose it is understandable that we have fled to the opposite extreme and invented myths to support our belief in planning. But if we wish to have a future landscape which has something of the texture and humanity, the *meaning* of the old, then it will have to be created with something of the same style – which was precisely 'a collation of haphazard suggestions by many people'. It will have to evolve slowly, as a result of the maximum possible community involvement. To be fair, the authors do finally acknowledge this, in the last two paragraphs of the book. They include a diagram of 'The Community Tree – still plenty of branches vacant'. It is clearly an elm, a species notorious for shedding branches at will. It is encouraging to see that one precarious low limb, ripe for sudden die-back, is labelled 'Landscape Architects'.

PART THREE

'Stumbling on Melons'

Between 1966 and 1973 I worked for Penguin Books as an editor. Our office lay alongside a branch of the Grand Union Canal and looked out over a bizarre urban-fringe landscape of factory wasteland, breakers' yards, rubbish tips and gravel pits. I became fascinated by the abundance of natural life that not only tolerated these places, but seemed positively to thrive in them. Lunchtime strolling soon developed into more concentrated exploration, and the end results were the book and TV film entitled 'The Unofficial Countryside' (1973). *The first of the following three pieces was a try-out of some ideas for the book.*

The Green Backlash
First published in *New Society*, 1 June 1972

Since this is the time of year for planning off-beat last-minute holidays, I would like to recommend, for those jaded by Himalayan lilies and Pyrenean alpines, a tour of the Thames estuary rubbish tips. I did the circuit by charabanc one wet Saturday last autumn, in the company of some loquacious master botanists, and can report that it made a holiday in the western Highlands a few weeks before seem positively barren.

The chief attraction – with one of those ironic reversals that often result from our efforts domesticate nature – was birdseed. The seeds of oil-bearing plants are now imported from all over the world by the companies that supply our budgie fanciers. Thence, via the cage floor, they find their way on to the rubbish dumps that sprawl over the waste ground near sizeable towns.

The soil in these places can be very congenial. It's kept open by regular bulldozing, drained and aerated by a skeleton of debris, and manured by household vegetable refuse, and for a few weeks every late summer, a rash of sub-tropical plants are able to flourish amongst the clutter.

Flowering on the Barking rubbish that day were cascades of love-lies-bleeding, sunflowers, gourds knobbly enough to ornament any Swedish fruit bowl, water-melons, maize and countless breeds of millet. Less prominent, but making up for this by their exquisite flowers, were flaxes and safflowers. Grubbing about for these smaller plants was no special hardship: these dumps are places where you unquestionably look down before you move a foot.

By no stretch of the imagination is this a substitute for a day in the country. You stand a fair chance of spraining your ankle, being covered by flies and finally asphyxiated by that inescapable, unmistakable rubbish tip stench. Yet no botanical garden was ever more fascinating than the spectacle of the persistence of these plants against every conceivable obstacle.

You never know what oddity is going to turn up next. Cannabis pops up here and there as an unintended ingredient of bird-food. Seeds from Australia and South America arrive here via wool-trade refuse (they were caught up in the fleeces back on the home range). You could probably guess which immigrant groups live in a tip's catchment area from the food plants growing there. In one dump in north Kent we found the plant from which they grow bean sprouts; in another, a virtually complete Indian spice garden – dill, fennel, coriander, fenugreek and cummin.

More curiosities. On a desolate tip behind the Ford works at Dagenham, where we had to be escorted by security guards (no hemp here, but hundreds of unregistered cars), there were acres of the villainous but magnificent giant hogweed. Back at Barking, we came across a thorn-apple, an old apothecary's plant much cultivated round London in the eighteenth century for its curious spiny fruits, used for asthma cures and love potions. It is still grown on a small scale by commercial drug firms and this could be where this plant originated. But it was just as likely to have been a genuine eighteenth-century relic: trials on the seeds of this species have shown that they are still fertile after forty years, and there is no reason why they should not be after two hundred.

The prize specimens on all rubbish dumps are the tomato plants. It would not have been difficult to gather dozens of pounds on each of the tips we visited – many of them already ripe and needing nothing more than a good wash. I think this would have tickled Ebenezer Howard, inventor of the garden city, who always believed that a town's green fringe should supply the bulk of its food.

Rubbish dumps could hardly be described as green belt, either by character or designation. Yet precisely because they have not been pampered, they often have a rural character (working farmyard crossed with marsh, maybe) missing from our doctored municipal parks. Ebenezer Howard's descendants have too often seen their green girdles as chastity belts, as much an excuse for keeping the promiscuous countryside out of the centres as containing urban flab.

But the countryside refuses utterly to be repulsed. It insinuates itself into any unguarded piece of ground, most especially those awkward-shaped bundles called 'marginal land'. The natural community quickly gets organized in these places, with its own development plans and its own solutions for a texture to counteract and contrast with the concrete. Plants and animals have none of our romantic preferences for picturesque backcloths. You are as likely to see foxes in allotments now as in well-keepered country estates. They have even been glimpsed in a Wandsworth cemetery, which will no doubt add to their reputation for knowing a sacrosanct wicket when they see one.

London, in fact, is an especially rich area for those who like a touch of the wild on their walks. The pink spikes of rose-bay willow herb have spread from the bomb sites, where they flourished after the Blitz, to adorn every railway cutting and parking lot in the city. Twelve pairs of herons nest in Regent's Park and last year cleaned out most of the ornamental goldfish ponds in central London. Badgers have a set in Kenwood. And nightingales have appeared, if not in Berkeley Square, at least in the disused East End docks.

For bird enthusiasts the real London attraction is probably Perry Oaks sewage farm, a huge expanse of bubbling sludge just at the edge of Heathrow airport. Here, in the spring and autumn, wading birds take time off from their migration flights to feast on the insects that thrive in the sludge. Some have come extraordinary distances, blown maybe 3,000 miles off a course that was meant to take them straight between north and south America. Come to this place at dusk, as the digging machinery starts to fade into the shadows, and you could be at the edge of the Wash at low tide. I'm not even sure if the arc lamps along the arterial roads and the constant roar of the planes overhead don't add an extra flavour, as those resilient birds also take off for their next refuelling stop.*

For those who would rather sacrifice the birds for the sake of a less malodorous walk, there are the 50-odd miles of London's canals, a totally different element even when the traffic is only yards away. Or there are the walkways that are being routed along some of the abandoned railway lines.

Of course, there are arguments against the delights of this unofficial countryside. Its landscapes are often smelly and almost always untidy. Yet they have something of the quality that makes Hampstead Heath, for instance, exceptional amongst London's open spaces. In most parks, the skinny poplar trees and geometric flowerbeds seem to have been modelled on the very planning developments they are meant to provide an escape from. But amongst the refugee spice plants, and the bouncy meadow grass and boggy dells of Hampstead, you can for a moment be in a world where urban man has been put in his place.

* Perry Oaks is now not open to the public.

Hyde Park

First published as part of a special issue on Hyde Park
in *The Sunday Telegraph* magazine, 9 October 1977

I noticed it almost as soon as I had scrambled clear of the traffic
in Park Lane. Not more than 30 yards inside the park an animal
was hanging motionless from a hawthorn branch, its head –
like a firing squad victim's – apparently encased in a bag.
Surely a keeper's gibbet in one of the Royal Parks was carrying
tradition too far? Then I moved closer, and a grey squirrel
exploded back into the bush, scattering nuts as it went. With
great self-possession it had been hanging upside down with its
head buried in one of the bird-feeders that are strung about the
park. On the ground beneath, pigeons and hedge sparrows
waited to pick up the spillings each time the squirrel panicked.

It would have been hard to imagine a more typically urban
episode. It was incongruous, opportunist and stylish, and set
me in the right frame of mind for my midsummer ramble.
There is, after all, nothing more incongruous than 600 acres of
imitation countryside slap in the middle of a city.

Yet Hyde Park is not really rural at all. If you try for a
moment to view it as a whole landscape, the illusion of riotous
greenery disappears. The trees are in rows, the grass shorn.
There are no inviting corners obscured by a rise in the land,
none of those sinuously logical tracks that a pattern of hedges
and hills marks out for you.

For all that, Hyde Park has probably the richest variety of
natural life of any of the central parks. Red admiral and
peacock butterflies haunt the Flower Walk dahlias. Tits nest in
the lamp standards along Rotten Row and wood pigeons in the
underground car parks nearby. It's popular with passing trade
too. Ospreys migrating over London have called in to fish, and
in 1970 two of those rare piebald wading birds, avocets, were
seen mincing along the edge of the Serpentine. There is even
some highly adapted human fauna: a man who listens in to the

85

calls of bats (which hunt for flies over the water) with a high-frequency receiver, and another who specializes in reading through binoculars the numbers on the rings of black-headed gulls.

So, with the prospect of much to look for, and a fine June day to do it in, I set out, thankful, like the squirrel, for anything that came my way. Much did. Chaffinches sang in the trees and young thrushes and blackbirds clucked less musically in the shrubberies. In the top of some tall lime trees a dozen juvenile crows loafed about and croaked for food. For the first couple of hours I stayed close to the Serpentine. Water is a magnet for birds and humans alike, and here both parties seem to have worked out an amicable relationship amongst the deck-chairs and rowing boats, the birds buying not only a diet supplement but a degree of human affection by agreeing to be fed. But it is a strictly limited tameness. Eight species of native water bird breed here, and when the pochard are diving for waterweed or the coots settling a territorial dispute, they are uncompromisingly wild. And out over the Serpentine Bridge there were birds whose lives are scarcely touched at all by humans. Swifts and house martins, which were absent from London for decades whilst the air was too noxious to support their insect prey, were skimming over the water to feed and drink, arching their wings above their backs to slow them down to a modest 30 mph. To a swift at full speed even the most beneficent bird lover must look like an extension of the concrete.

But away from the water less was happening. I began to wish rather strongly for a change in the texture of the grass, for a patch of daisies or a tree which had not been fastidiously shorn of every branch below 10 feet. The most unnatural thing about a park landscape is its lack of bushiness, which is the natural successional stage between grass and trees. I once heard of a park keeper in Highgate who explained that the official hostility towards undergrowth was 'to prevent dirty practices in the bushes'. Rampant scrubbiness amongst the well-bred ornamentals; it would indeed mean more work for the gardeners, and an extravagant new breed of litter. Yet Hampstead, up in the hills, does not seem to have become a sink of iniquity; and I wonder how much the rather prim layout of Hyde Park is a product of nothing more than the thoughtless tradition of regimentation that underlies every geometrically planted municipal bed.

Yet manicured and formally arranged though they may be, there is a multitude of trees in the park, something over 200 species it's reckoned. One of the best in Kensington Gardens is the Tree of Heaven (*Ailanthus altissima*), which is becoming naturalized in many of London's most inhospitable waste-lands. It has great clusters of nectarous cream flowers, which are believed to be responsible for the muscat-flavoured honey which occasionally crops up in Kensington beehives. The elms, sadly, are dying here as everywhere else, and when all other remedies fail they are cut down. But at the end of the nineteenth century, seven hundred mature elms were re-moved from Kensington Gardens as casually as if they were litter. They were the tallest trees in London, and the home of a vast rookery. There was talk of disease, but none was found when they were felled; and the real explanation for this extraordinary act of official vandalism appears to be that the ground beneath the trees became muddy and untidy during the winter. Attitudes, it seems, haven't changed much in a hundred years.

Hyde Park's trees are fewer and more widely spaced than those in Kensington Gardens, but it has a good selection of exotic oaks and limes. But the most *treeish* tree, a real hunk of gnarled wood with a bark like braided ships' hawsers, grows close to the Dell. It's an Asian relative of the walnut known as a Caucasian wing-nut. Most town trees – and the ethereal London Plane is a case in point – are planted for purely architectural reasons, for the ornamentation provided by their foliage, or the formal contrast they make with buildings. But this wing-nut, also no mean looker, was a tree you could get to grips with. The trunk separated into flutings at the base, just wide enough apart to sit between, and the leaves, which were festooned with long chains of pink and green flowers, drooped to within 5 feet of the ground. In its shade it was cool, comfortable and cosseting, and if the view had been anything more exciting than the back end of Hyde Park Barracks, I would happily have stayed there the rest of the afternoon. I'd certainly had enough of rather aimless meanderings, which increasingly seemed the wrong way to explore a place with no real vistas and a great deal of human traffic. I needed a pitch.

In the end I lighted upon the enclosures at the end of Longwater. The Serpentine narrows down to a thin strip here, and the bordering vegetation has been allowed to grow relatively unchecked. Or unchecked by humans, at least, for what intrigued me here was the sight of a flock of grazing rabbits. They were wild ones, to judge by their colour, though once I glimpsed a jet black one, and in another thicket a venerable grey beast as long-haired as an angora. These no doubt had escaped, or been dumped by bored pet-owners. There is also some traffic the other way. One of the gardeners told me that children have been sneaking the babies home for pets. It sounded a rather sorry trade, but a preferable way of keeping the population in check, perhaps, than myxomatosis. At their current levels, the rabbits, grazing selectively alongside the ducks, have succeeded in producing something that has eluded the lawnkeepers – real flowery meadows, carpeted with buttercups and bird's-foot trefoil, and the odd clump of ox-eye daisy and red campion.

These little pastures with their miniature flocks were the centre of attraction in this corner of the park. Tourists photographed them, children hurled food in at their inhabitants. One 5-year-old girl was offering up the chips from her takeaway lunch. Somewhat taken aback by the rabbits' utter indifference, she offered the congealed lumps to the mallards. 'Anybody?' she pleaded. When even the pigeons shied away in disgust, she gave up and ate them herself. Then she started throwing in the hamburgers. . . . No wonder there are all those stories about the park ducks becoming belligerent. To judge by the voraciousness with which they attacked those pink slices, they have all become carnivores.

The sun shone on, the evening rush-hour began, and I sat down on a bench for a last look over Longwater. Blackcaps and willow warblers, here for the tourist season from Africa, sang in the thickets. A great crested grebe swam past with a large candy-striped youngster in tow. And on the far bank a heron, perhaps from the Regent's Park colony, made a few perfunctory dashes at the Serpentine's eels and feral goldfish. Then, bored or frustrated, he waded out into the water and *wallowed*, up to his chin. When he had finally dragged himself back to his look-out perch, he looked like a wet sheepskin rug, hung up to dry. Crocodiles of ducklings and goslings swam about directly underneath – with some temerity, I thought. I have seen a heron swallow a young moorhen, live and whole, and I would not put anything past them. But this one sat me out for more than an hour, rocking peaceably on the branch in something remarkably like a Lotus position. He was, I think, just drying out and enjoying the sun, like the dust-bathing sparrows and the basking ducks.

Hyde Park's two cultures – holiday camp round the Serpentine, playgroup in Kensington Gardens – are reflected, and perhaps in part created, by their natural life. In both areas wildlife and humans jog along together with mutual tolerance, a good deal of improvisation, and something that can only really be described as goodwill.

Oxford: City of Greening Spires

First published in *Harper's & Queen*, May 1983

'It is typical of Oxford,' said Charles Ryder to Sebastian on their return from Brideshead, 'to start the new year in autumn.' Typical, too, that the city's oldest monument isn't some august monastic foundation but the pleasantly scruffy stretch of pastureland known as Port Meadow; and that this home of lost causes and high brows should have begun the popularization of Morris dancing, after it was rediscovered, alive and kicking, amongst the Headington 'Quarry Roughs' whose ancestors had dug out the building stone for the colleges.

Oxford has a hopelessly ambivalent relationship with all things earthy and natural. Famous for a bracing and sceptical intellectual climate, it is also notorious for dank and enervating airs. Its acres of lawn and water generate an almost irresistible aura of perpetual garden-partying, yet you still feel that your attention should be concentrated on higher things, like Gothic cornices or the Logical Positivists. (And 'Is paying attention an action or a state of mind?' is just the sort of question they like to wrangle over.)

When I was 'up', as the apt expression goes, I was so overawed by the headiness of it all that I quite forgot I was a country boy who'd spent most of his youth mooching about the hedges with pockets full of squashed plants and Romantic poetry. My rural roots grew back, I'm glad to say, but surprised me by putting out some strong tendrils towards this beguiling city. Now I'm beginning to believe that Oxford's tolerance of almost any flight of fancy – when by rights it ought to feel prickly and unsettled from so many clashes of class and opinion – has a lot to do with being thoroughly infiltrated by forms of life vastly older than the crustiest fellow or Bodleian incunabula.

If you stand on a high point near the outskirts of the city and the sun is bright enough to pick out its honey-coloured stonework, Oxford looks like a collection of so many village churches. The vaunted spires seem to be growing out of a continuous thicket of green, a huge rectory garden. It isn't a mirage. Both city and university are embedded in an ancient, intricate and often ecclesiastical countryside. If your view is from the west, it would be over the ragged flats of Port Meadow, which was well organized as common grazing long before Domesday. The Freemen of Oxford still put out cattle on it, and it is one of the last stretches of grass in lowland England never to have felt the plough.

Another is the group of hayfields tucked alongside the A40 to the north. Pixey and Yarnton Meads are a unique survival of a communal system of land tenure that flourished in the Middle Ages. They are what is known as 'lot-meadows'. The local commoners don't own any particular strip, but simply the right to take a certain proportion of the hay crop. What they literally possess is a share in a number of ancient cherrywood balls inscribed with names like Watery Molly, Perry and Dunn (probably corruptions of medieval family names). Up until a few years ago the balls were still ceremonially drawn by lot to decide who had which strips of hay that summer.

In the thirteenth century the meadows were nominally owned by Godstow Nunnery, whose shell survives in a field near the Trout Inn. In this territory near the city boundaries you soon become aware of the influence of the female church in the Middle Ages. The meadowland in nearby Binsey, for instance, was the property of St Frideswide, a twelfth-century princess who is the patron saint of the university. To the east of the city is the imposing bulk of Brasenose Wood, given to the Prioress of Littlemore by Henry III as a source of fuel for the priory. Now it is part of Shotover Country Park, and Oxford City Council manage it with great sensitivity as the kind of coppice-with-standards that the Prioress no doubt ran – and use the cut wood in rustic architecture all over the city.

It was out of – and over – this complex alloy of theology and husbandry that there grew the jumble of cloisters, quadrangles, halls, laboratories, temples to Christ and memorials to Lord Nuffield that together make up *Universitas Oxoniensis.* No wonder that reminders of the old order sometimes shoot back up between the seams. Amongst the ruins of the nunnery at Godstow there grows one of the few surviving English colonies of a curious plant called birthwort. Because its yellow flowers look something like a uterus in shape, birthwort was popular as a gynaecological herb, and was introduced to monastic physic gardens in the twelfth century. (It does indeed speed up labour, and one distinguished Oxford botanist, the late E. F. Warburg, believed that its presence at so many nunneries may have hidden a multitude of little sins!)

Oxford is infused by greenery as well as lapped by it. Plants scale the walls, arch over the alleyways, spring out of the thinnest cracks in the stonework. Sometimes they even force their way through it. In the 1880s a root of the ivy that then covered Magdalen Tower found its way into the college wine cellar, broached the cork in a bottle of port, and drank the lot.

All this lush and promiscuous growth helps soften the edges of the city which is a labyrinth of nooks and crannies. It turns backyards into courtyards, and waste plots into improvised gardens. And what makes so many of these patches doubly exciting is that you only catch sight of them as tantalizing flashes: a fellows' garden sparkling through a half-open gate; dark shrubs straining against the railings at the end of a one-way street; something very like a clump of young trees growing out of the *top* of a pollard willow. . . . Then your punt floats on, the gate closes, the traffic lights change. In the busiest part of St Aldate's Street, one architect in tune with the spirit of the place has generously designed a courtyard gate with a large port-hole cut out of its middle.

Oxford's alleys and walled lanes are crucial to this sense of a city insinuated, though they had a rather bad image in the past. Thomas Hardy's Jude saw them as an impossibly decrepit framework for 'modern thought' – 'obscure alleys, apparently never trodden now by the foot of man . . . their extinct air being accentuated by the rottenness of the stones'. Max Beerbohm called New College Lane a 'grim ravine', and though I suppose this is topographically accurate, it is precisely the lane's quality as a kind of overground underpass that makes it the most dramatic back-way through the city. Its secret, I suspect, lies in the tall walls not *quite* cutting off the world outside. They are crowned with self-seeded snap-dragons, wallflowers and tiny yew trees, and just above and behind these, the mysterious tops of things: a row of runner beans, a frieze of gargoyles round an invisible quad. A hand appears, picks a bean, and vanishes again. There is one corner in the lane where the angles of the half-hidden roofs and trees seem to break all the rules of perspective. It is like looking at one of those two-dimensional geometric illusions and you begin to appreciate how Lewis Carroll, otherwise a mathematics tutor called C. L. Dodgson, was able to conjure up the quirky world of Alice here.

As well as these stone arteries, there are the waterways. Oxford is surrounded and penetrated by rivers and sits on a bed of impervious clay. It is under siege by water, which at the slightest excuse reclaims its old territories, flooding meadows and lawns alike, and sometimes seeping up through the pavements. When the Cherwell is in full spate, the crush of punts by Magdalen Bridge looks like a scene from Hong Kong harbour. I remember one February day when even the ducks could not swim against the current, and Magdalen gardens were graced by the spectacle of snowdrops flowering under-neath the water.

The college gardens are, of course, the pride and glory of green Oxford. There are forty assorted colleges and halls, and probably four times that number of discrete gardens. There are knot gardens, herb gardens, formal French gardens, and all manner of scholarly garden conceits. In New College there used to be a living sundial, with the numbers clipped out of box, and a continuous avenue of trees each with its bottom limbs grafted on to those of its neighbours. In University College there is still one bewitching corner where a solitary bush of deadly nightshade grows against an inscrutably worn stone.

Worcester College is famous for its swans and lily-decked ponds, Wadham for its wildness, St John's for its rockery (into which various Presidents have slipped plants gathered on their Aegean holidays). Trinity has long shaded lawns, much used for croquet and play-reading – though for enterprising employment of grassy space it would be hard to beat the occasion on which a full symphony orchestra, including live cannon, played the 1812 Overture in Christ Church's Tom Quad.

If you wander through the modest gateway of St Edmund Hall, into the little paved courtyard with its pots of bright red geraniums hanging from the walls, you might be forgiven for thinking you had strayed into a discreetly modernized coaching inn. In New College it is more like a castle, with dense herbaceous beds banked up to the massive wall the college shares with the city. The medieval city wall reappears (now rather sadly scoured of wild flowers) as one of the boundaries of Merton College gardens, and along its top runs an avenue of lime trees and a rose-lined lovers' walk. Next to Merton is Corpus Christi, with the most delightfully bizarre garden of all. Corpus has a reputation as something of an ark, having given sanctuary at various times to a vast swarm of bees (which were reputedly faithful to the Professor of Rhetoric's roof until Cromwell dissolved the monarchy), a mascot fox in memory of the college founder Richard Fox, three tame owls, and two tortoises painted with the college colours. And in the front quad, Charles Turnbull's elaborate 1605 sundial is topped off with a pelican. So you may be prepared for the botanical follies that greet you in the surrounding beds, and for a herbaceous border that might contain – to pick just a couple of square yards – sweet peas, sweet corn, pansies, passion flowers, borage, rue and a cabbage. This cheerful green-grocer's mix (which looks, I must stress, wonderfully exuberant and not at all contrary) continues as you move into further quads, past little thickets of catmint, gooseberry, climbing roses and lovingly hoed urban weeds, until you reach a kind of summit near the city wall, where a potting shed and bed of pumpkins look almost directly into the elaborate east window of Christ Church Cathedral's Lady Chapel. It is not really as incongruous as it sounds, and this is the way that plants must have jostled together in monastic gardens, before they were so rigidly separated into the useful and the decorative. (And much like George Eliot's description of her perfect garden, where 'you gathered a moss rose one moment and a bunch of currants the next; you were in a delicious fluctuation between the scent of jasmine and the juice of gooseberries'.)

The most celebrated and serene of all Oxford's gardens is at Magdalen College, whose emblem, fittingly, is a madonna lily. Magdalen's 100 acres are in a more orthodox style than the conceits of Corpus and New College, and may remind you of the grounds of several stately homes; but no other college has anything quite like its wistaria-draped cloisters and its riverside walks, and especially its deer park amongst the trees.

The deer seem to get tamer by the year and have taken to loitering winsomely near the railing when there are tourists about. Perhaps they have a herd memory of the time when it was a favourite undergraduate prank to intoxicate them with lumps of sugar soaked in port – though I suspect this is a rather better type of snack than they are being fed at present.

As for the long circular walk around Magdalen Meadow, it is so wild and bosky that you may find it hard to believe you are only half a mile from the city centre. But then the college's great tower floats into view between the trees, you notice blue alpine anemones amongst the white natives and snakeflowers in the grass, and remember where you are. Such gentle and artful deceptions are the essence of Oxford's landscape, and much of their charm is due to the fun they make of labels like 'wild' and 'domesticated'. It would be a brave person indeed who tried such categorization on the plants in the vicinity of Magdalen Meadow. From the huge trusses of mistletoe that make the poplars look as if they are in mid-winter leaf, down to the meekest creeping periwinkle, they are all growing with wild abandon; but are quite likely to have nipped in here from the Botanic Gardens, just across the High Street.

This, founded in 1621, is the oldest botanic garden in Britain; and being small, decorous and high-walled is the most tranquil of sanctuaries in which to pass a summer's afternoon. But it has a long history of escapes, including the one and only flower to be named after the city, the Oxford ragwort. Linnaeus introduced this European species to the Gardens in the mid-eighteenth century, and its downy seeds appear to have made their breakout sometime during the 1790s. They soon arrived at the station, and appeared to find the wide swathe of ground that had been cut out to accommodate the Great Western Railway much like their rocky native terrain. Using the spreading road and rail systems as its own freeways, the footloose ragwort (which had been disparagingly named *Senecio squalidus*) rapidly colonized the rest of England. The Victorian botanist Claridge Druce once wrote about a railway journey he shared with a party of its seeds, which floated into his carriage at Oxford and out again at Tilehurst, 20 miles down the line.

Such is the casual way that many Oxford products spread themselves about, and the ragwort might be considered the city's most apt botanical emblem – were it not now strewn so liberally across the whole of urban Britain. All manner of plants have been suggested for this honour, especially some of the city's notable trees. The gigantic oak against which Magdalen was built, and which could reputedly shade 3,456 men, fell down with 'a violent rushing noise and a shock felt throughout the College' on the night of 29 June 1789. But the youngish sycamore jutting into the High Street, which the town planner Thomas Sharp called the most important single tree in Europe, is still standing. So – though only just, given the tipsy angles at which their trunks grow – are the ancient mulberry trees with which so many of the colleges have been endowed since the time of James I, and whose fruit still occasionally finds its way into High Table sorbets. Horse chestnuts would also have to be highly listed. Luscious trees spread over many of the alleys, especially the cobbled lane between Brasenose and Exeter Colleges. And Christ Church meadow would be a bleaker place without its chestnuts now that the great elms in the Broad Walk have been felled.

But individual trees, I think, are too mortal and too recently arrived to qualify as Oxford's companion plants. We need proof of a more continuous presence, and of roots in a dimmer past. Godstow's birthwort is just the kind of thing, and by no means the only obstinate floral relic of ancient ecclesiastical habits (heresies are easier to root out than some of these herbs). The snakeshead fritillary, whose mottled purple bell-flowers colour parts of Magdalen Meadow in late April, may be another – although it is popularly supposed to be wild, and has been the most celebrated flower in Oxford poetry. What is odd is that it wasn't recorded here until 1785. It's hardly conceivable that such striking and gregarious blooms weren't noticed if they were already growing here – even allowing for the fact that the Professor of Botany in the late eighteenth century was the somnolent Humphrey Sibthorp, who only gave one lecture in forty years. The most convincing explanation of their origins that I have heard is that they were introduced to the Meadow from genuinely wild colonies in Ducklington in the Windrush valley. This living was in the patronage of Magdalen College, and it's quite possible that an incumbent (paying an all too rare visit to his parish) took a fancy to the fritillaries and carried a few corms back to Oxford.

But my own choice for an emblem would be the greater celandine. It is an unprepossessing plant, rather like a small-flowered yellow poppy, but it grows in almost every corner of the city, at the edges of car parks, on ancient walls, in waste plots and at the foot of exclusive college staircases. Its leaves are also unmistakably carved on the shrine to St Frideswide, which dates from 1289 and now sits in the Lady Chapel at Christ Church. It's an unusual plant to find portrayed on sacred medieval stonework, and its presence here may not be a coincidence.

Greater celandine was anciently introduced to Britain from southern Europe, as a physic herb. The orange latex which can be squeezed from its leaves was used as a caustic, to cauterize warts and – harrowing thought – to clean 'away slimie things that cleave about the ball of the eie'. Now Frideswide, as well as being the patron saint of the university, also happens to be a benefactress of the blind and was canonized chiefly for summoning up a holy well whose water had curative powers for the eyes. (The story would make a wonderful plot for a romantic novel: Frideswide was the daughter of a twelfth-century Mercian princess and went into hiding for three years to avoid an arranged marriage. Her luckless suitor subsequently went blind and Frideswide, in an act of contrition, entered holy orders. Then up sprang the well, at Binsey, just down-river from Oxford.)

I like to think that the celandine was carved on her shrine as a pagan tribute to the supposed power of her well. Eyewash, perhaps. But the shrine is worth a look anyway. Its carvings are amongst the finest representational portraits of plants that survive from the thirteenth century, and there are beautiful and precise figures of ivy, columbine, hop, maple, sycamore (the earliest known representation in Britain), jack-in-the-green hawthorn and both species of native oak.

The fabric of Oxford has always been decked up as much by its citizens as by nature itself. All over the city flowers have been carved on stonework and painted on the walls of dining halls. Literal gardens have been planted up wherever there is space, from the foot of St Mary's Church, eight centuries old, to the yard of the Turf Tavern with its log-burning brazier.

And no wonder, for there are still tensions in this city which need easing. It is still a place of privilege, and Town and Gown are still wary of each other's territories. As for the cloister-and-quad model – the archetype of civilized pedestrian precincts and housing estates – it has been all but ignored in most of the city's ghastly new developments.

It would be hard to prove the good done by Oxford's greenery, but it helps to provide some reassuring continuity in a city that is forever replacing much of its younger generation. And the parks and rivers are great social levellers. Oxford's commons in a way. A punt on the overgrown reaches of the Cherwell is no place to stand on your dignity, and it is hard to lounge about in flower-draped alleys with anything other than goodwill. Above all, exuberant growth puts pomposity and logic in their place. As Jan Morris, in her incomparable book about the city, write about the siting of that supreme scientific monument to plants, the Botanic Gardens: 'The designers so arranged things that if you stand with your back to the urn beside the southern wall, and look down the central pathway to the ornamental gate, over the lily pond, through the ceremonial pillars and across the fountain – if you look down this bower of the Age of Reason, Magdalen Tower is *not* framed in the centre of the great gateway.'*

* *Oxford*, Faber & Faber, 1965.

PART FOUR

'Green Thoughts...'

The Wild Garden

First published as an introduction to *The Wild Garden*
by William Robinson, Century, 1983

The Wild Garden is not William Robinson's masterwork (that is *The English Flower Garden*, published thirteen years later in 1883) but it is fast becoming his best-known title – literally, one might say, since the phrase is now a rallying call for a host of gardeners and conservationists who have never read a word of Robinson's text. What's joined them is a shared hostility towards the regimentation of living things, be it in the formalities of the Victorian garden, or the rigours of the new countryside beyond the pale. The revival of this old idea has led to some curious alliances, the principles which Robinson pioneered in some of the grandest English gardens, for instance, now guiding the planting of abandoned shunting yards and New-Town parks.

There are more ironies about the circumstances in which this book has come into its late inheritance. 'Wild gardening' sounds such an absurd contradiction that it runs the risk of seeming just another piece of fashionable urban whimsy. Yet it was developed in the nineteenth century precisely to challenge fashionable gardening styles. Robinson was concerned above all else to enliven stuffily formal gardens with ideas – and plants – from a still comparatively unplundered nature. It couldn't have occurred to him that wildness itself might one day become an endangered quality that people would want to recapture in their gardens, and his own view of the book's emphasis is plainly stated in its subtitle: 'The Naturalisation and Natural Grouping of Hardy Exotic Plants with a Chapter on the Garden of British Wild Flowers'. In advertising a later edition in 1881 he drops the wild-flower note altogether and substitutes 'being one way onwards from the Dark Ages of Flower Gardening, with suggestions for the Regeneration of the Bare Borders of the London Parks'. Yet even here we can glimpse the common ground between Robinson's borders of artfully rowdy perennials and modern suburban corners abandoned to nettles and butterflies. It is the conviction that naturalness as a *process* (not the static, contrived naturalness of the eighteenth-century 'landskip') is an aesthetic, even an ethical, virtue.

Of course, dark ages and bare borders still rule the more conservative public parks. But when Robinson was a young man, learning his trade on the Ballykilcavan Estate in Northern Ireland, they were almost universal. That curious mixture of extravagance and earnestness that characterized the Victorian era had found perfect expression in the fashion for what came to be called 'carpet bedding'. Tender and often rather garish flowers from Imperial outposts were laboriously raised in greenhouses, planted out in dead straight rows and symmetrical formations (with the exact spaces between each plant kept quite bare for contrast), allowed their brief season of brilliance and then ripped out again. Gardeners were not so much plant stewards as drill sergeants. It was as if, as Robinson put it, they were carrying 'the dead lines of the building into the garden'.

The challenge which he made to this enervating system, and which became his lifetime's mission, is given its first airing in *The Wild Garden*. The book necessarily presents the argument in a specific and limited context, but it contains the essence of Robinson's whole philosophy. Like all great and abiding ideas this was bold and simple. It was that gardens, as the abodes of plants, should be places for celebrating their life and liveliness, the ways they naturally mingled and spread in impromptu mosaics of colour and form. Robinson loved the *rightness* of plants allowed their natural settings – pure lemon globeflowers in a dark, damp hollow; the unprompted hedginess of a wild rose scrambling over a fence – and the way that flower and shrub, moss and fern 'relieved' each other. Wild gardening, being a way of fostering the natural groupings of plants, also involved a way of looking at their convivial growth in the wild.

*   *   *

William Robinson published *The Wild Garden* when he was 32 years old. He had been writing about his ideas and travels for the previous seven years, and in these reports and articles it's possible for us to see his developing eye, as he begins to forge a philosophy of cultivation out of an experience of nature.

His spell at Ballykilcavan was short, unhappy and probably decisive. He hated the vast greenhouses with their trays of seedlings being nurtured for the 'floral carpets', the wasteful nonsense of a system in which flowers were pulled up only to be planted again, and in which a garden was bare earth for half the year. He left in 1861 when he was 22 years old, under rumours (appropriate but probably untrue) that he had marched out of the greenhouses leaving the windows open, the fires out, and great carnage amongst their inmates.

William was a conspicuously talented as well as ambitious young man, and had no trouble finding a responsible post in the Royal Botanic Society's garden in Regent's Park. From here he was despatched to gather plants and gardening ideas all over northern Europe. Every new place, new garden, even new bed set off in him sparks of excitement and inventiveness. One of his first visits was to the great Fernery at Backhouse near York, where there was an artificial ravine, 20 feet wide, drenched with cascades of water and a profusion of ferns: 'To one like myself, fresh from the region where monotony holds an almost undisputed sway; where "decided" colours take a too decided lead, the relief afforded by this exquisite touch of nature, and sudden collapse of pot, bench and regulation, could only be equalled by a sudden transfer from a Bedfordshire Cucumber field to a Gentian-covered Alp.'* At the age of 26 he already had the originality of taste and facility of language to be able to pun with that unexpected, exact word 'decided'. He knew the precise word to set against it too, when he described Veitch's famous nursery in Chelsea and 'the mystery and indefiniteness which constitute beauty of vegetation in its highest sense'.

By now he was contributing regularly to journals such as *The Gardeners' Chronicle*, praising the massed primroses at

* Mea Allan's biography, *William Robinson 1838–1935: Father of the English Flower Garden*, Faber, 1982.

Cliveden and the cyclamens naturalized amongst moss and violets (and beautifully set off by them) at Vilmorin's house near Paris. It was his receptivity to these kinds of association, especially those which were accidental, that enabled him to turn his ideas into a practical strategy for garden design. He had seen how the lumpiness of paeony bushes was softened by growing them amongst long grass; how a weeping willow could be transformed by the drapery of a Virginia creeper, especially in the autumn sun; and in a remote burn in Linlithgowshire, how naturalized musk could make the thinnest trickle of water glitter. Tramps through the Lake District and the Alps inspired him with ideas for rock and wall gardens. In a bleak chasm in the Saas valley he saw wild houseleeks for the first time, growing in the smallest crevices and crowding in great cushions across the boulders. If they could survive to brighten this forbidding habitat, why shouldn't they do the same on sunbaked walls and garden paths?

Impressions and designs entwined in his imagination, until he had enough raw material for a whole book on naturally inspired planting schemes. As luck would have it, he was already friendly with his publisher John Murray, and had been asked to prepare a plan for his garden in Wimbledon. Never a man to miss an opportunity, Robinson kept his intentions a tantalizing secret even from his patron:

It may not be amiss to remark that the scheme we are preparing is utterly unknown to gardeners and therefore you must not be surprised if your man does not at first enter into the spirit of it . . . I despair of fully explaining my meaning until I get the idea explained in a book, or, better still, till one or more gardeners show the system in perfection.

Murray happily rose to the bait, and published *The Wild Garden* the following year in 1870.

The book's impact during the years that followed is best judged by how commonplace are some of Robinson's quintessential 'indefinitenesses'; drifts of naturalized daffodils alongside grassy drives, jungly bamboos half hidden in shrubberies, a clematis tumbling over a pear tree. Or commonplace in large gardens, at least. Robinson makes it clear that his ideas were intended principally for those who owned what we would call 'grounds', who had meadows, lakes, spinneys, plantations, parks, unruly extremities that were decidedly not part of the 'outside room'.

Those with ordinary-sized plots were to get their inspiration from his later book, *The English Flower Garden*. But fragments and echoes of the specific ideas in *The Wild Garden* continued to resurface until the recent upsurge of interest in ecology suddenly gave them a new relevance. Robinson always was just as much an ecologist as he was a designer, a maker of artefacts. 'The true garden,' he wrote, differs 'from all other arts in this, that it gives us the living things themselves and not merely representations of them'. If that liveliness was suppressed a garden was no different from an inanimate building. So Robinson kept faith with the natural rules by which plants lived, associated, competed, spread, reproduced and succeeded one another.

But equally he saw that simply to mimic nature would be to make the whole idea of gardening superfluous. His solution, whilst adhering absolutely to his principles of ecological design, was to contrive *new* natural groupings – compressed, condensed, perhaps deliberately contrasted – and to combine plants that the accidents of geography kept apart in the wild ('exotic' in his subtitle simply means anywhere in the temperate zone). It was simply a matter of the best use of the land. It would take centuries of waiting and acres of ground to re-create in a garden the effect of a wood awash with bluebells (and why bother, since there were so many peerless examples in nature?). But the *principle* of naturalizing springtime bulbs under trees or in unmown grass was attractive, economic gardening. So why not a few dog's-tooth violets or American wood lilies (*Trillium* species – 'very singular and beautiful') under the lilacs instead? And why not native wild flowers in areas where these also were unfamiliar or scarce? On the southern chalk downs Robinson had seen the dramatic effect of tiers of brooding yews draped with the white plumes of traveller's joy (which he liked to call virgin's bower). It was a combination which would grace any garden – though so

would variations on the same theme: a deep-red rose insinuated through a holly, or a hop on a hawthorn.

The greatest tribute to the strength of Robinson's ideas is the
degree to which they are now being built on and translated in
quite new situations. The creed behind *The Wild Garden* can be
seen, for instance, in the practice of sowing native wild flowers
– now increasingly 'exotic' even in their own districts – inside
gardens; in one aspect of the cottage garden revival, where,
with typically eclectic modern taste, carefully tended Victorian
roses might be underplanted with a naturalized layer of that
great favourite of Robinson's, the white musk mallow; and in
the experiments under way in some public parks in 'ecological
management', in which, for reasons of economy as well as
appearance (and how Robinson would have approved of the
pairing of those goals), natural groupings of hardy native
shrubs and flowers needing next to no maintenance are being
established.

But perhaps what would please him most is the way that,
here and there, such groupings are establishing themselves. It
is a delicious, ironic tribute. Two of his best-loved flowers,
golden rod and Michaelmas daisy, thrown out of gardens
precisely because their powers of naturalization are a sight too
wild for most gardeners, have taken up residence on mainline
railway embankments, and are now spreading in spectacular,
mottled, billowing sheets – exactly how their champion felt
they should be seen. For in the end, Robinson's most important legacy to us is that he helps us to *see* plants afresh. After
reading this book it is hard to look at any wild plant without
seeing its garden potential; or, for that matter, to see felicitous
garden arrangements without enriching one's understanding
and appreciation of the society of plants in the wild.

Gilbert White

First published as the introduction to the Penguin English Library edition
of *The Natural History of Selborne*, by Gilbert White, 1977

On 24 November 1822, on one of his rides through the back-
waters of Hampshire, William Cobbett passed a turning for a
village whose name sparked off a faint memory:

> I forgot to mention, that, in going from Hawkley to Greatham, the
> man, who went to show me the way, told me at a certain fork, 'that
> road goes to *Selborne.*' This put me in mind of a book, which was once
> recommended to me, but which I never saw, entitled *'The History and
> Antiquities of Selborne'* (or something of that sort) written, I think, by a
> parson of the name of *White*, brother of Mr *White*, so long a bookseller
> in Fleet-street. This parson had, I think, the living of the parish of
> Selborne. The book was mentioned to me as a work of great curiosity
> and interest. But, at that time, the THING was biting *so very sharply*
> that one had no attention to bestow on antiquarian researches. Wheat
> at 39s. a quarter, and South-Down ewes at 12s. 6d. have so weakened
> the THING'S jaws and so filed down its teeth, that I shall now
> certainly read this book if I can get it.

Cobbett did not take the fork on that occasion. But one of his
readers sent him a copy of *The Natural History and Antiquities of
Selborne, in the County of Southampton,* by the Rev. Gilbert White
which had been published thirty-four years before. True to his
word, Cobbett read it, and was sufficiently affected to make a
special trip to White's parish the following autumn (1823). He
loved Selborne, which was 'precisely what is described by Mr
White. . . . Nothing can surpass in beauty these dells and hillocks and hangers.' And like every pilgrim since, he searched
out the 'curiosities' which White had written about with
such easy vividness, zig-zag path, the hollow way, and the

churchyard with its ancient yew. 'The land,' he wrote, 'is good, all about it.'

Nothing captures more perfectly the anomaly of White's book than the transition between the nonchalance of Cobbett's first note, and the respectful passion of his second. Both, in their own ways, are entirely reasonable responses. Considered at its face value, the book *was* something of a phenomenon. How could the jottings of a rural parson about the goings-on in an unknown Hampshire village have such an effect on all who read them? How was it that a collection of letters on local natural history – for that is all there is to the book – written with wilful parochialism at a time of social revolution in France and agricultural upheaval at home, became the fourth most published book in the English language? There had already been at least four editions of the book by the time Cobbett was writing. By the 1970s the new editions and translations numbered in excess of two hundred. The early cheap versions were carried all over the world by expatriate Englishmen, sick for the dells and hillocks of home. It is worshipped by American naturalists, who have never seen half the creatures White talks about, and by the Japanese, who have seen even fewer.

It's no wonder that the search for a key to White's appeal has preoccupied his critics and editors – sometimes to the point of obsession, as if there were some stylistic mannerism, some trick of words, which, properly decoded, would reveal the secret. There is not, of course; and the book's strength lies more in its refreshing ingenuousness than in any contrivance. But though it won't, thankfully, be explained away, it must be seen in perspective. Perhaps more than any other single book it has shaped our everyday view of the relations between man and nature. I say 'everyday' without in any way meaning to belittle White's scientific contributions. These were considerable, particularly in the area of observational method. But their impact on scientific theory was small, and they were soon overshadowed by the discoveries of giants like Darwin and Mendel.

White's contribution was more personal, in both senses. He was perhaps the first writer to talk of animals – and particularly birds – as if they conceivably inhabited the same universe as human beings. In White's chosen patch, the village of Selborne, they did so literally. Listen to this passage on the swift. White is writing in the summer of 1774 from his house in the High Street, just across the village square from the church where he was curate:

It is a most alert bird, rising very early, and retiring to roost very late; and is on the wing in the height of summer at least sixteen hours. In the longest days it does not withdraw to rest till a quarter before nine in the evening, being the latest of all day birds. Just before they retire whole groups of them assemble high in the air, and squeak, and shoot about with wonderful rapidity. But this bird is never so much alive as in sultry thundery weather, when it expresses great alacrity, and calls forth all its powers. In hot mornings several, getting together in little parties, dash round the steeples and churches, squeaking as they go in a very clamorous manner; these, by nice observers, are supposed to be males, serenading their sitting hens; and not without reason, since they seldom squeak till they come close to the walls or eaves, and since those within utter at the same time a little inward note of complacency.

(*Letter XXI to Daines Barrington*)

This is a new note in nature writing – and not just because of the accuracy and percipience of the observations. White is plainly talking from his own experience. His swifts are real, not 'bundles of responses', or links in some taxonomic chain. They are living birds in a living situation. With no more than a hint of anthropomorphism, White suggests that their lives have a richness and rhythm of their own. And by describing them on a summer evening in a particular English village, he is able to awake in us the possibility of a human response to them.

If this seems unexceptional today, it's partly a result of White's own pioneering. He was living at the tail-end of the Enlightenment, and his work was both a product of and a response to the spirit of the age. Eighteenth-century science was dizzy with its own advances and was dominated by systematists like Ray and Linnaeus whose overriding desire was to find (or drill) some order and sense of hierarchy into the teeming ranks of Creation. One consequence of this was that most naturalists retired to their laboratories, trying to fit the bewildering new collections of exotic plants and animals sent back to Britain by the colonial explorers into some coherent scheme of things.

White, by contrast, was predominantly a field-ecologist. He was more interested in the relationship between living animals than between their 'taxonomically significant parts', and once wrote to Daines Barrington that 'system should be subservient to, not the main object of the pursuit.'

But this is no more than rephrasing the problem. How was this unexceptional country parson able to go against the whole tenor of science in his time, and rise to such a position of eminence in both natural history and literature? What moved him to keep such meticulous records of his observations, and craft them – with more purposefulness than is obvious at first sight – into a book of a kind which was quite new in the natural sciences? And what was the bond that drew him back so persistently to that tenacious Hampshire village?

Selborne – 'a stream through the sallows'. It is impossible to talk about White outside the context of the village in which he lived and died. Selborne was the source of his inspiration, and has become a memorial almost equal in stature to the book it inspired. When you look at the village – and it has changed very little in the last two hundred years – it is not difficult to see why White loved it, and how it was so easily and winningly immortalized. In many ways it is a thoroughly ordinary settlement: a single main street with a few side lanes, lined with cottages that are neither dull nor excessively picturesque. There is a green next to the church (the Plestor, which had its own maypole in White's day), a couple of pubs, and an old butcher's shop across the street from White's house. But Selborne lies cupped in a bowl formed by a confluence of soils and streams, and the countryside immediately around it is, without exaggeration, idyllic. A steep beech-clad hanger rises just behind the village. Rich pastures spread out towards the north-east, and beyond the church there is a jumble of dells and copses ringed by a perpetual clamour of rooks. In an hour's stroll you can pass through oak forest, chalk downland, sandy heaths, water-meadows, hop fields, and a pattern of agriculture that seems scarcely to have been touched by the revolutions of the last two centuries. Selborne, in short, is the landscape of the pastoral dream made flesh: cosseted, balanced, endurable, a condensation into a single parish of almost every type and mood of scenery to be found in lowland England.

That this is the place where White lived is, in one sense, the only important fact in his biography. He was born in the vicarage on 18 July 1720 and died 100 yards away in The Wakes on 26 June 1793. He never married, and remained a country clergyman all his life. Everything that happened to him, by decision or default, seemed designed to preserve his single-minded commitment to his native village. His father, John, was a barrister, but he was an exception in a family otherwise almost exclusively dedicated to the Church. His grandfather (also called Gilbert) was vicar of Selborne, his mother a clergyman's daughter, and most of his uncles and nephews had livings in neighbouring parishes. The pressure on him to follow in their footsteps must have been considerable, though at no stage did he show any dissatisfaction with his calling.

In 1727 his grandfather died and the whole family moved across the Plestor to the house now known as Wakes. White went to schools in Farnham and Basingstoke, and even at this comparatively early age began to keep spasmodic records of his natural history observations. Before he was 11 he was planting out his own trees in the grounds of Wakes.

At the age of 19 he went to Oriel College, Oxford. He seems to have been a normal, perhaps even hearty, undergraduate, and whatever sensitivity he was to develop later in his life was certainly not apparent then. He rode, hunted, shot and fished with almost ferocious vigour. Ironically – given what was to become his consuming passion – he used to gun down small summer migrants to keep his hand in for the winter shoots.

He became a fellow at Oriel in 1743 and spent the next fifteen years travelling around England, returning continually, and with apparently increasing devotion, to his native village. He could never become vicar of Selborne (the living was with Magdalen College, not Oriel) and during this period he took

up five temporary curacies, three of them at Selborne. His
Oxford colleagues were forever tempting him to apply for
positions at Oriel, but only once, apparently, did he succumb,
when he unsuccessfully applied for the Provostship. His beloved village was too strong a magnet, and in 1761 he settled
for the curacy of Farringdon. This village is only 2 miles from
Selborne, and White was able to carry out his duties from
Wakes. He kept this position for twenty-four years, and in
1784, on the death of the incumbent at Selborne, finally
became curate of his birthplace for the fourth time, a position
which he held until his death.

He led, by all accounts, a quiet and relatively leisurely life.
He never scrimped his clerical duties, but with only a few
dozen marriages and burials to attend to a year, he had plenty
of free time to pursue his natural history. Nor did he ever
permit his religious persuasions to distort his reasoning. There
is no trace in his writing of moralizing about 'brute creation', or
of the mawkish search for natural parables that fill the books of
the Victorian parson-naturalists. And, as men of God go, he
enjoyed his share of earthly pleasures. There is even a touch of
the mannered aesthete about him. He was especially partial to
composed views and Gothic follies. There is a delightful
description in Letter XXXVIII to Daines Barrington of one of his
friends discovering the echo in Galley Lane: 'At first he was
much surprised, and could not be persuaded but that he was
mocked by some boy; but, repeating his trials in several
languages, and finding his respondent a very adroit polyglot,
he then discerned the deception.' It is slightly surprising that
White didn't seek to preserve the echo by keeping its 'object' (a
hop-kiln) clear of foliage, for the superficial topography of
much of the village is a result of his landscaping. His garden,
'outlets' and meadows stretched along the base of the hanger.
Up its steep slope he helped build the famous Zig-Zag path,
and at the top a hermitage in which he held summer picnics.
One of the uninvited guests one evening was a nightjar:

You will credit me, I hope, when I tell you that, as my neighbours
were assembled in an hermitage on the side of a steep hill where we
drink tea, one of these churn-owls came and settled on the cross of

that little straw edifice and began to chatter, and continued his note for many minutes; and we were all struck with wonder to find that the organs of that little animal, when put in motion, gave a sensible vibration to the whole building!

It is likely that he found this visitation just as bewitching as those of the flighty Battie sisters, and of the one person it has been suggested he had a romantic attachment to – 'Hecky' Mulso (she nicknamed him 'Whitey-bus'), the sister of White's close friend and mentor, John Mulso. But the relationship came to nothing, and as Rashleigh Holt-White put it, White 'had but one mistress – Selborne'.

It's no real wonder, then, that White's first serious writings took the form of a *Garden Kalendar*. This was a diary of the principal events in the horticultural year, which he began in 1751. By 1768 he had expanded it into a more general 'Naturalist's Journal', which covered records and observations of the natural world as well as the garden. He was encouraged in this by the explorer and naturalist Daines Barrington, who that year had sent him one of the special diary blanks he had had printed up by White's brother, Benjamin. White immediately began filling it with his daily observations on weather, flowers and the comings and goings of birds, and continued almost without a break until four days before his death. The manuscript of these journals in the British Museum gives a fascinating insight into the development of White's interests. The early entries are disciplined and terse, each note on barometric pressure and 'trees first in leaf' neatly confined to its own narrow column. But as White's skills in observation and imaginative reasoning develop (and perhaps the first plans for a book start to form), so the records and observations start to trespass outside their columns.

White met Daines Barrington in Benjamin's bookshop in May 1769 and began to correspond with him one month later. But he had already started the formal correspondence which was to form the *Natural History* two years earlier, with the eminent zoologist Thomas Pennant, whom he had also met in Benjamin's shop. It's difficult to appreciate now what an intellectual lifeline correspondence must have been to country-dwellers in the eighteenth century. All road transport was slow and hazardous (White was additionally cursed with acute coach-sickness), and though letters went by the same routes, at least they could be sent more frequently. White complains more than once of the lack of neighbours with whom to discuss natural history, and the pleading for information in some of his letters to his brother John in Gibraltar reveals an unashamed and impatient yearning for the exchange of knowledge and ideas.

The first mention of the possibility of a book based on White's journals and letters is in his note to Daines Barrington of 12 April 1770. Yet there are clues which suggest White may have been thinking of publication for some time, and that with a flash of editorial flair, he had seen that a series of letters, datelined Selborne, was the form that would most exactly convey the idea of a parochial ecology. They would pin together time and place, and the sense of a continuing flow of life.

He carries the motif as far as to top and tail the collection of real letters (discreetly edited) with a number of mocked-up letters in the style of the rest of the book. And in 1773 he writes to a friend: 'Pray tell me over again the story of the swallow building on the dead owl's wing, and on the conch, etc; I think I could make good use of it.' The information was supplied and subsequently worked into Letter XVIII to Daines Barrington. These are more the kind of moves one would expect from a shrewd working writer than some innocent rustic scribe.

Nevertheless, eighteen years were to elapse between the first mention of the project and the delivery of the manuscript – a delay brought about by what White's friends regarded as his incurable procrastination, and by his insistence on compiling a rather dull appendix on the antiquities of Selborne. But in December 1788 Selborne at last had its *genius loci* laid bare in print. And the immemorial quality of that village found itself reflected in a book which not only endured itself, but, by a kind of symbiosis, helped the village to endure too. One of the *Natural History*'s most reassuring qualities is the sense it gives of an unbroken line of continuity in the life of the countryside. Two of the lime trees that White planted to hide the blood-

stained forecourt of the butcher's shop are still standing.
Swifts still arrive in the village in the first week in May and fly
round the steeples in much the same numbers as were counted
by White. Helleborines bloom on the hanger, and golden
saxifrage in damp ditches by the lanes. The 1,000-year-old yew
continues to have its barely perceptible annual growth re-
verently charted. (Even Cobbett put a tape round it, and found
that 8 inches had been added to its 23-foot girth since White's
day.) From our embattled modern countryside it is curiously
heartening to look back and see that White, too, had to wrestle
with the problems of heath fires, vandals and venison
poachers. Even as I write this, southern England is in a state of
extreme drought, and the Forestry Commission is broadcasting emergency fire warnings for Hampshire. Two hundred
years ago to the day, White wrote in his journal for 30 April
1776: 'Birds silent for want of showers . . . no rain since the
beginning of March.' Life goes on. Yet if White had a strong
sense of the invariables of natural life, he also had a sense of
occasion and, even more, of place.

The place for which he had the greatest feel was, of course,
Selborne. There were not many others that he really knew.
Whilst Cook and Banks were botanizing on the other side of
the world, and his correspondent Pennant was leading an
expedition to the Hebrides, White was watching bats over his
lawn. He never travelled further than Derbyshire, and was so
overcome by the size of the Sussex Downs that he referred to
them as that 'vast range of mountains'. He was bound to, and
by, Selborne. It was his manor and he surveyed it on horseback
like a benevolent squire, attentive to the lives of all its inhabitants. Other men, more in tune with the expansiveness of the
times, might gaze briefly at migrant birds in tropical skies. But
White had watched them in their nests, and even, on occasion,
held them in his hands. He had 'gently insinuated' field
crickets from their holes on a grassy bank just 300 yards behind
the church. He knew the exact length of the bounds of his
parish.

I have used that word 'parish' many times already. It seems
to me crucial to understanding the impact of White's writing.
He was parish priest. He talks in the very first sentence of his

book of his desire to write a 'parochial history'. (David Elliston
Allen, in a memorable phrase, has described Selborne as 'the
secret, private parish inside each one of us'.) 'Parish' is a very
laden concept. It has to do not just with geography and
ecclesiastical administration, but with history and a system of
loyalties. For most of us, it is the indefinable territory to which
we feel we belong, which we have the measure of. Its boundaries are more the limits of our intimate allegiances than lines
on a map. These allegiances have always embraced wild life as
well as human, and show themselves no more explicitly than
in the universal delight at the annual return of the 'village'
birds – the swifts and swallows and martins. I don't think it is a
coincidence that these were White's favourites too. But his
originality lies in the way he wedded a celebration of these
thoroughly irrational parochial loyalties to sharp and dispas-
sionate observation. It is this blend which is the quintessence
of what we know as 'natural history', and which makes it a
different kind of knowledge from biology. It has survived even
into these days of scientific rigour. Town and village floras are
still published, and birds still harried across county boundaries
so that they can be added to local tallies. It hardly needs saying
that these artificial territories have little scientific significance.
But, lovingly watched and logged as they are, they help
provide a common ground for wild life and human feeling,
and we must thank White for that.

His writing style was parochial too. In the very best sense of
the word he was a gossip. He delighted in telling stories about
his own and others' observations (though never about himself). He writes rivetingly about a raven dashed to her death as
the tree in which she was nesting, and which she refused to
desert, was felled; about an extraordinary shower of gossamer
on the district; about the moose which he made a special visit
to Richmond to see, but 'was greatly disappointed, when I
arrived at the spot, to find that it died . . . on the morning
before'. He examined it meticulously, but the poor beast was
already putrefying and White had to cut short his studies:
'From the fore-feet to the belly behind the shoulder it
measured three feet and eight inches: the length of the legs
before and behind consisted a great deal in the *tibia*, which was

strangely long; but in my haste to get out of the stench I forgot to measure that joint exactly.'

This sentence is pure White: eager, precise, unaffectedly witty, and scrupulously honest. Nowhere in his work does he trust absolutely in anything other than his own observations. When he refers to another's opinions or records he invariably makes it clear he is quoting. He is not afraid to rebuke scientists as distinguished as Linnaeus and Scopoli for their occasional gullibility and lapses of discipline. Writing to Daines Barrington about the contentious behaviour of the woodcock, he says:

Faunists, as you observe, are too apt to acquiesce in bare descriptions, and a few synonyms: the reason is plain; because all that may be done at home in a man's study, but the investigation of the life and conversation of animals, is a concern of much more trouble and difficulty, and is not to be attained but by the active and inquisitive, and by those that reside much in the country.

White, out on his rounds with a notebook always in his pocket, was all of these things, and this is why he was able to make so many original contributions to British natural history. He distinguished between our three summer leaf-warblers. He discovered the harvest mouse and, in Britain at least, the noctule bat. A hundred years before Darwin, he realized the crucial role of worms in the formation of soil. He was one of the very first naturalists to understand the significance of territory and song in birds.

But White's unique contribution to natural history lies less in the catalogue of species and concepts that he added to the textbooks, than in the style of his perception: *how* he saw, and how he communicated what he saw. Let me quote a rather lengthy passage about house martins to illustrate this:

About the middle of May, if the weather be fine, the martin begins to think in earnest of providing a mansion for its family. The crust or shell of this nest seems to be formed of such dirt or loam as comes most readily to hand, and is tempered and wrought together with little bits of broken straws to render it tough and tenacious. As this bird often builds against a perpendicular wall without any projecting ledge under, it requires its utmost efforts to get the first foundation

firmly fixed, so that it may safely carry the superstructure. On this occasion the bird not only clings with its claws, but partly supports itself by strongly inclining its tail against the wall, making that a fulcrum; and thus steadied it works and plasters the materials into the face of the brick or stone. But then, that this work may not, while it is soft and green, pull itself down by its own weight, the provident architect has prudence and forbearance enough not to advance her work too fast; but by building only in the morning, and by dedicating the rest of the day to food and amusement, gives it sufficient time to dry and harden. About half an inch seems to be a sufficient layer for a day. Thus careful workmen when they build mud-walls (informed at first perhaps by this little bird) raise but a moderate layer at a time, and then desist; lest the work should become top-heavy, and so be ruined by its own weight. By this method in about ten or twelve days is formed an hemispheric nest with a small aperture towards the top, strong, compact and warm; and perfectly fitted for all the purposes for which it was intended.
(*Letter XVI to Daines Barrington*)

This is a remarkable passage, not just because of White's ability to interpret the reasons behind birds' behaviour, but because of its *precision*. The exactness of his observations and of his language are inseparable. The martins, for example, do not just use 'grass', but 'little bits of broken straws', an image that is at once more sympathetically evocative of the energetic activities of these little martlets, and also more helpful in understanding how they actually put their nests together.

White has often been criticized for the lack of attention he pays in the book to his human parishioners. Richard Jefferies wrote that:

He knew the farmers and squires; he had access everywhere, and he had the quickest of eyes. It must ever be regretted that he did not leave a natural history of the people of his day . . . . The gallows-trees grew far too plentifully at the cross roads in those days, and the laws were inhuman, men were put to death like wild beasts: in fact they seemed to look on a man as a species of wolf that could only be tamed by stretching its neck.

This scarcely sounds like the same world that White describes. Yet, to tell the truth, there is a kind of animal quality about the few humans that do cross his pages. They are curiosities, like the bat and the moose: a leper, a mad bee-boy, gypsies, a toad-witch. They are described objectively, but with little of the sympathy or respect that White shows for his favourite wild creatures. They are not met on their own terms.

There is no suggestion of malice here, or even of aloofness. By all accounts White was a sociable and easy-going man, and much liked by his parishioners. I think it is simply that, although he brought the natural world closer to the human, he did not take the next step, and see that human affairs were in their turn part of the natural scheme of things. If White had known what we know about the unity and fragility of life on earth, he would have passed down to us a much less comforting book. For him the living world was beneficent and infinitely renewable. That was a matter of faith. On the day of the storming of the Bastille, he was busy writing a whole page in his diary on the nesting habits of the night-jar.

In rescuing natural history from the dusty cabinets of the taxonomists, White had given it a human scale and a human setting. Whether he had 'humanized' it is another matter. In some ways he simply helped make man's 'dominion over nature' social as well as intellectual and physical. Knowledge was still a goal that overrode compassion, and White had few scruples about sacrificing the lives that delighted him in order to gain it. Yet I believe he was beginning to be touched by the kind of sympathies that did not come fully into the open until half a century later, in the writings of men like the poet John Clare. White loved his creatures, yet was unsure how to convey this emotion except by affectionately accurate description. He experiences regret, wonder, joy, grief, but is diffident about working these feelings openly into the details of what he observed. The force of this suppressed emotion helps, I think, to explain White's obsession with the problem of whether swallows and their kind returned en masse to Africa, or whether some of them spent the winter with us in 'hybernaculums'. He never resolved the problem, for he never found the evidence his high scientific principles demanded for the resolution of a question. But for thirty years he was preoccupied by migration and hibernation. He demanded records from his correspondents, poked about in likely holes in rocky lanes, and hired men to scour the winter bushes for sleeping birds. He raises the issue in half of the letters to Pennant and Barrington, and in one exchange it's clear that he is being partly driven by sheer frustration at his inability to fill this yawning gap in science:

When I used to rise in a morning last autumn and see the swallows and martins clustering on the chimnies and thatch of the neighbour-ing cottages, I could not help being touched with a secret delight, mixed with some degree of mortification: with delight to observe with how much ardour and punctuality those poor little birds obeyed the strong impulse towards migration, or hiding, imprinted on their minds by their great Creator; and with some degree of mortification, when I reflected that, after all our pains and inquiries, we are yet not quite certain to what regions they do migrate; and are still farther embarrassed to find that some do not actually migrate at all.
(*Letter XXIII to Thomas Pennant*)

But it is the admission of that 'secret delight' in the possibil-ity of 'hiding' that lingers in my mind. And as the subject is aired in letter after letter, it begins to look as if White simply did not *want* the swifts and swallows and martins to go. Such was his loyalty to his village, and to these 'parish' birds that magnanimously shared its streets and steeples for the sum-mer, that I think that in an unscientific corner of his heart he hoped that a few might stay there with him for the winter. And is it being too fanciful to read in his reference to Goree (an insignificant island off the west coast of Africa) as one of the wintering quarters of his martlets, an example chosen because of the slight distastefulness of its name?

White never openly admitted feelings of this kind in his book, and the sadness is that two centuries of less gifted nature writers, looking to him as a model, have made concrete that apparent separation between fact and feeling. But it's doubtful if White himself – for all his restraint and self-effacement – saw objectivity and delight as contradictory. There is an entry on the arrival of the first swallow of summer in his journal for

1768, the excitement of which no cold Latin objectification can disguise. It reads simply:

April 13: Hirundo domestica!!!

First published as an introduction to *Gilbert White's Year*,
Scolar Press, 1979

The earliest surviving record of Gilbert White's lifelong passion for journal-keeping is in a manuscript diary kept by his future brother-in-law, Thomas Barker, of Lyndon Hall in Rutland. On 31 March 1736 it notes that 'a flock of wild geese flew N.', adding – presumably in acknowledgement to the observer – the initials GW. The future author of *The Natural History of Selborne* was 15 at the time, and probably spending the Easter holidays with his uncle at Whitwell Rectory, 2 miles away. There is nothing special about the observation – except, for a boy perhaps, its rather austere clarity. But the habit of noting, which was also a way of seeing, stuck. Increasingly White's life seemed to be structured around, and for that matter *like*, his diary. It was inquisitive, tidy, industrious, without excess or indulgence, and conducted with an almost sacramental attention to the details of climate and the seasons. To within a fortnight of his death he went about the duties of living and the business of writing with the same measured discipline, summing up the day in his little secular collects. On 10 June 1793 he cut five cucumbers and read the funeral service over 'Mary Burbey, aged 16'. On 21 June it was 'Bright, sun, golden even. Cut *eight* cucumbers . . . . Many swifts.' The next day he 'Cut *ten* cucumbers. Provence roses blow against a wall. . . . ' By the end of the month, in the middle of a desperate drought, Gilbert White's name had joined Mary Burbey's in Selborne's parish register.

Although he was not to become permanently installed as curate of Selborne until 1784, White lived at the family house (Wakes) in the village for most of his life. His first position after ordination in 1747 was as curate to his uncle Charles, who was rector at Swarraton, 10 miles away. He stayed there two years and then took up a succession of curacies, all within easy

121

reach of his home. None of these positions was very demanding and during the week White was normally able to stay at Wakes. Although his father was still alive White appears to have been in charge of the garden even by the late 1740s, and in 1751 he began the first of his formal journals, the *Garden Kalendar*. In a book of cheap quarto letter paper, stitched together by hand, he recorded the chief events of his horticultural year, the sowings and flowerings and pickings, the changes in weather and yields, the introduction of new crops and the alterations in the structure of the garden. White was deeply involved in the contemporary revolt against the formal French style of gardening, and in the growth of interest in more 'natural' landscaping (itself part of a wider debate about man's place in nature). Yet what is especially fascinating is the way his garden innovations proceed simultaneously on two different, and by no means obviously consistent, fronts. On the one hand, there is the scrupulous scientist, experimenting with new strains of vegetables and cultivation techniques, worrying about efficiency and productivity, and recording the results of every project with meticulous accuracy; on the other hand, the aesthete, constructing an extravagant and picturesque estate of arbours and follies but recording it all with the same precise voice. It was an instance of an ambivalence that ran right through his life. He made trials of crops which were then scarcely known in Britain – sea-kale, maize, potatoes, even wild rice – and developed a sophisticated heating system for his forcing beds. Meanwhile, beyond the vegetable plots, he was indulging in the Picturesque and building a massive ha-ha, a device consisting of a wall hidden in a deep ditch which kept cattle out of the garden (but still in the view) without spoiling the prospect from the house: 'The mason finish'd the dry wall of the Haha in the new garden, which is built of blue rags, so massy, that it is supposed to contain double the quantity of stone usual in such walls. Several stones reach into the bank 20 inches' (24 January 1758).

In 1768 the *Kalendar* begins to peter out as White had by now started the more comprehensive 'Naturalist's Journal' (see page 113). Soon, however, the entries in the journal start to stray beyond the topics that would normally be regarded as part of a naturalist's field of interest. He records important foreign affairs, notes what sounds very much like an epidemic of Russian flu (2 June 1782) and describes the appearance of hot-air balloons over Selborne with the same relish and rapt thoroughness as he would a swift, a meteor, or a new kind of mobile garden ornament. His taut style (it is not playing with words to call him a journalist) had a way of making all occurrences appear like natural phenomena. The one conspicuous exception are the events of his own emotional life. In more than 15,000 daily entries it is hard to find a single one which can be interpreted as an explicit reference to White's feelings. Despite this – though perhaps because of it – their imaginative strength and *implicit* emotional content can be very powerful and clear.

It is possible to read the journals as a simple historical record of natural events, and spanning more than forty years with scarcely a break, they are probably unique in their continuity. Yet it is their sharp and lucid poetry that is White's most important legacy. Stripping away conventional pastoral allusion, adjectival excess; self-examination, searches for meaning, he distilled a form of spare, literary miniature which had an immediacy not seen in this kind of English prose before: 'Women hoe wheat. Gossamer abounds. Sowed a bed of celeri under a hand-glass.' That was the morning of 19 March 1787. The next autumn (30 October) 'Larches turn yellow; ash leaves fall; the hanger gets thin.' In three phrases he can catch the essence of a single afternoon or a whole season.

Yet it's doubtful if White himself saw his journals as 'literature'. For him, I think, they were more a kind of intellectual ledger, a place to take daily stock of the world. They have a persistent, probing quality that lifts them beyond merely passive records or exercises in wordcraft: 'Thatched roofs smoke in the sun; when this appearance happens rain seldom ensues that day. This morning they send up vast volumes of reek' (14 November 1777). The tone and structure of this entry aren't really those of a casual diary entry. The details are too carefully selected and ordered, as if they were part of the answer to a larger, unspoken question.

White's apparent objectivity disguises a wealth of deep

feelings towards natural life, and if his scientific curiosity shapes his observations, so too does the fact that he was a pre- or embryonic Romantic, and then again a man who had chosen to live and work in a real community rather than retreat to the abstractions of the laboratory or the imagination. It was out of the interplay and mutual discipline of these different ways of perceiving that the sharpness of his journal prose comes. It is his *choice* of detail, and of a language in which to describe it, that marks him out as more than a scientist. As a student of meteorology he is fascinated by the appalling winter of 1786; but it is equally as a writer that he chooses to say of it 'Meat frozen so hard it can't be spitted' (4 January 1786).

Turned on to human behaviour, his sympathetic gaze can pick out quite startling images, the effect of which is the greater because we suspect it to be uncontrived: 'The twigs which the rooks drop in building supply the poor with brush-wood to light their fires' (18 March 1775). At face value it is a straight-forward account. But for us, living after the Romantics, it is all but impossible to read 'straight' – purged of symbolism and poignancy. And on this occasion White too is aware that he has recorded an image with a more potent frame of reference than usual. Drawing on the only modes available to him for the explicit exploration of allegory, he adds an orthodox pastoral footnote: 'Thus did the ravens supply the prophet with neces- saries in the wilderness.' There was probably no more than a few minutes between the making of the two entries, yet they are centuries apart in their feeling: the observation – vivid, particular, almost modern in its unornamented realism; the gloss – stiff, generalized, conventional. Luckily White did not comment upon many of his notes. Like Coleridge and Hopkins after him he is best in his first, immediate impressions, and as a result he has been able to leave us an unparalleled celebration of moment, just as *The Natural History of Selborne*, in its more considered way, is a monument to place.

James Fisher

First published in *The Times*, 23 June 1978 as a review of *Watching Birds*, by James Fisher (revised by Jim Flegg), Penguin

At the time of his tragic death in a car accident in 1970, James Fisher was involved in research on the fossil birds of Britain. It was typical of him to be ferreting away in such an obscure corner of scholarship whilst, under another hat, helping to energize the movement that turned conservation into a popular cause that year. He had done another brilliant balancing trick four years before under the unlikely cover of *The Shell Book of Birds*, in which he had guided his readers through the bird lore of tenth-century Irish monks and the Anglo-Saxon riddle poems.

James Fisher was one of the last of what they used to call natural philosophers, a man who deplored specialization as a way of life as much as superficiality as a way of working. Equally at home with poetry as with a microscope, he saw language as just one of the gloriously rich resources to be found in a life-sciences laboratory. He was, as it were, a scientist by faith. He admired passion, but detested slovenliness. It was the poignant realism of John Clare that attracted him more than the aesthetic musings of W. H. Hudson. Above all, he admired Gilbert White for his gifts of lucidity and precision.

This book – which fittingly takes it chapter headings from White – was one of the first Fisher wrote, and in it you can see the unadulterated, crusading scientist more sharply than in any of his later books. He wants his audience to share not just his enthusiasm but his *discipline*, and the combination generates a wonderful clarity of style: 'We must remember that not only special kinds of beaks but beaks in general are adaptations. A wing is an adaptation for flying. An egg is an adaptation for nourishing the young.' With the same kind of openness he goes on to talk about subjects as arcane as taxonomy and population cycles. Yet the excitement, the mystery, is always there, as when he is talking about migration: 'It is always sobering to remember that in seven grammes of chiff-chaff is centred a navigational computer capable of guiding the bird not only to the same country, but to the same county and the same copse, when it returns next season.'

It is a measure of the sway Fisher held over a whole generation of ornithologists that it is difficult to tell where his original text merges into Jim Flegg's excellent updatings. This accessibility – as a style and a goal – was the essence of what Fisher was about. He was a democratic scientist, and in that respect radically different from the patronizing school of nature writers that preceded him, and from the many contemporary biologists who sound as if they would like to put the natural world under lock and key. Fisher not only believed that everybody had the right to enjoy birds, but they could all play a useful part in the process of studying them. This was a rare point of view in 1940 – and perhaps from the hand of a 28-year-old at the beginning of a war, an heretical one. Fisher's own view of the cultural importance of a continuing involvement with the natural world is forcibly expressed in his original preface: 'Some people might consider an apology necessary for the appearance of a book about birds at a time when Britain is fighting for its own and many other lives. I make no such apology. Birds are part of the heritage we are fighting for.'

Life on Earth

First published in *Vole*, April 1979 as a review of *Life on Earth*, by David Attenborough, Collins

On the cover of *Life on Earth* there is a photograph of a Panamanian tree frog peering out towards the watching world. It is wide-eyed, alert, exquisitely fragile, the optimistic face of new life. It has about it something of the look of the encapsulated embryo that drifts out into the galaxy at the close of Kubrick's film *2001*, only it seems altogether more amiable. Unquestionably, this frog is friendly.

David Attenborough took this photograph himself, as he did many of the other pictures in a book which is no less remarkable than the series it accompanies. I must confess that there were times during the television programmes when I was overcome by a surfeit of biological variety. Such a teeming parade of wonders, oddities, extravagances. . . . It seemed both too glib and glossy – some kind of global circus – and too tidily explained, as if evolution were not just an abstracted concept but a machine, manufacturing products to an inexorable plan.

Reading the book gives one time to catch one's breath. David Attenborough explains very firmly in his introduction that he does not regard the procession of life as purposeful in any way; but that talking about evolutionary change as if it were something *achieved* by animals is a convenient shorthand, and avoids filling the book with endless teleological qualifications. Thus released from the remorseless march forwards, one is given a new insight into the excesses of nature, and into the nature of excess. Extravagance is the way of the world, it is what life on earth is all about. Leaves are invented and instantly fray at the edges, split into pairs, change colour, stay on, drop off. Feet grow knobs and spikes with the abandon of an animated cartoon; but they come in useful sooner or later, for gripping branches, balancing upright on the ground, poking, pulling, playing the guitar. You take your pick.

The point about natural selection is not that it picks the best, but simply excludes the unworkable. In nature, anything that doesn't actually fail, goes. A natural world designed by modern planners would have none of the redundant embroidery of the one we live in. Peacocks would be scaled down to the drabness of turkeys, birds of paradise would not dance and sing upside down in trees.

The major fault in our retrospective view of evolution is to confuse use with purpose, in the way that an historian using the evidence of Edwardian photos might deduce that the point of the little finger was to balance the weight of tea-cups. David Attenborough demonstrates how, time and again, inventions in the natural world are entirely fortuitous. They are improvisations, contraptions, new tricks with old equipment. The reptilian archaeopteryx was blessed with excessively shaggy scales that happened to be sufficiently feathery for it to be able to glide about from branch to branch. Birds had been invented. The sweat of skunks – like all animals, they perspire when they are afraid – is so foul that it helped drive off whatever was the source of threat. The smellier the skunk the better its chances of survival. The sweat of the duck-billed platypus, on the other hand, is very rich in fat, and its sweat glands came in handy for feeding its young. The first nipples were on the way.

If all this reinterpretation were being done consciously we would be tempted to call it art. Or perhaps a set of brilliant puns. Perhaps both. Certainly the closest analogy to whatever process it was that led the angler fish to use an extended fin-spine as a luminous bait, is what was going on when Marcel Duchamp hung a lavatory seat in an art gallery. The photograph of the angler fish, like many of the other startling images in the book, is suggestive of an infinity of new, bizarre variations. In many ways these still photographs – not resolved along particular paths of action as they are in moving films – are more expressive of the *potentialities* of living forms. You can see the first glimmerings of the whole range of new emotions in the ecstatic eye of a jay, caught in the act of anting just for the fun of it.

But eyes – now they're the kind of invention that makes you pause. Scales and sweat glands are one thing; but how on earth do you move from a single photosensitive cell to an image-forming, percept-making, *seeing* eye in a few hundred million years? Those who have tried the sums, who have attempted to estimate the numbers of mutations, selections, improvisations and adaptations that would be necessary, have found that the discrepancies are just too great. Some process in addition to selection pure and simple must have been involved if these highly complex structures were to be perfected in the time available.

David Attenborough does not write with the metaphorical dazzle of some other biological popularizers, but in the unobtrusive elegance, humour and sense of wonder in this book it soon becomes clear what his own image of natural evolution is. It is very far from the brute struggle for survival that is the conventional view of Darwinism. Life on Attenborough's earth is collaborative and creative. Species get together to work out solutions to life's problems more often than eliminating each other. Lichens, for example, are symbiotic associations between a fungus and an alga. The Portuguese man-of-war is a whole community of essentially different organisms swimming under one roof. A colony of termites is such a complex association – from the protozoa that live in their guts and help digest the wood they eat, to the fungi they cultivate for auxiliary food – that it would be no surprise if it went one stage further and developed the power of movement, like some gigantic crustacean. There are many biologists who believe that even the nucleated cell as we know it today is a result of the coming together of a collection of previously independent organisms. Was that first eyed creature, 500 million years ago, formed in this way, by a marriage of mutual convenience between a free-floating colony of photosynthesizing cells with lens-like skins, and a blind trilobite?

Attenborough's world is also a communicative one, where animals watch, mimic and learn from one another. It is a delight to find a natural history book which ends with a whole chapter devoted to man, the best at this particular activity. Yet such have been the 'creative achievements' of other organisms in the field of communications that the only unique accomplishment Attenborough will allow *Homo sapiens* is the making of pictorial and symbolic *representations* of the world. But he will not let us totally out of the ring even on this account. He describes human culture, unforgettably, as 'extra-corporeal DNA', an allusion that is all the more riveting when you consider how often the snake-like creation gods of early people are drawn entwined like a double helix.

Attenborough's account of his own encounter with a truly uncivilized people (the Biami in New Guinea) is the most enchanting episode in the book. He seemed to communicate most successfully with them by expressive movements of the eyebrows – a facility which followers of the author's television career will know to be wonderfully evolved in him.

The natural world's cleverest survival tactic – if I can use the shorthand for a moment – may have been the development of proto-Attenborough, people who began to enjoy nature for its own sake. The fully-evolved version – which has the facility to travel 1,500,000 miles round the earth in three years, and produce a stunning demonstration in film and print that variety is not just the spice but the elixir of life – is the kind of creature that could turn the 'struggle for survival' into a red herring.

First published in *The Times*, 19 January 1978, as a review entitled 'Masterful Unravelling' of *Inheritance and Natural History*, by R. J. Berry, Collins

Genetics has never had a good public image. Fraught with awful possibilities and saddled with a fanatical fringe of racial 'improvers', it often seems more like one of the black arts than a science. Bernard Shaw was one of the few popular writers who seem to have understood the delightful capriciousness of biological inheritance, and when Isadora Duncan asked him to have a child with her because his brain and her body would make such a wonderful combination, replied, 'Yes, the snag would be if it had your brain and my body.'

R. J. Berry, Professor of Genetics at London University, is four square behind Shaw, and has written, in this latest New

Naturalist volume, a remarkable celebration of *difference*, in the context of our native plants and animals. Modern genetics is not an easy science, knitting as it does just about every discipline from higher maths to ancient history; and it is a privilege to have it unravelled so masterfully amongst the familiar forms of whelks and field mice. Yet of all the many virtues of Professor Berry's book – its wit and elegance, its marvellous rummagings, its great common sense – I would value very highly the fact that it is not *over*simplified. The biochemistry, for instance, will remain impenetrable to all but biochemists, though it is an essential part of the story. The editorial preface quite courageously recommends skip-reading, and it is a pleasure to be able to do this to some effect for once.

As for the stories, which even the most amateur naturalist will not want to skip, they build up a compelling picture of the inventiveness of natural evolution. Their message is that survival depends on variety. Every species – indeed, the planet's whole 'living community' – is forever trying out new variations and experimental models, which may eventually find their niche, guard against a change in climate or food supply and help keep the thread of life going. There are genes which influence not only physical characteristics like wing colour and seed size, but complex factors like territorial loyalty and population control. One of the most recent additions to our list of breeding birds, the collared dove, was able to expand its range because of a genetic change in its temperature tolerance.

Yet no mutation or inherited capability is any use unless it 'fits' a particular set of environmental conditions (which do, of course, also influence the development of individual organisms directly). This is where natural selection comes in. Our cuckoo population, for instance, is grouped in highly specialized local tribes, each laying in the nest of just one species – which is a habit *learned* by the young cuckoos because of the choice made by their parents. The genetic component is the size and colour of the eggs. The more they resemble the hosts', the less likely they are to be deserted.

If types like this are physically isolated – by, for instance, being marooned on an island – they will begin to form new inbreeding subspecies, like the sixteen distinct races of field mice which breed on our offshore islands. If they drift back again, their unique collection of genes will be added to the mixing pot, producing new – and, quite possibly, successful – combinations. Scarlet tiger moths (unlike humans) actually 'prefer' to mate with individuals genetically distant from themselves.

It is their gain, just as the whole contemporary trend towards uniformity could well turn out to be our greatest loss. I wish Professor Berry's quiet but irrefutable arguments about the importance of the gene bank could be read by every genetic engineer who thinks he knows better than millions of years of natural experiment, by every 'developer' who thoughtlessly drives another species closer to extinction, and by every EEC bureaucrat who seeks to outlaw another vegetable variety. The biosphere has survived this far by hedging its bets against every eventuality, not by imagining it already had all the final answers. Professor Berry's profoundly important book is a worthy addition to the eco-system, being in its form just as much as its theme an expression of the diversity of creation, and an excellent subject for natural selection.

I first became aware of Richard Jefferies' ambivalent literary reputation in the mid-fifties. My adolescent reading had been dominated by Jefferies' nature writing and for years my school English essays contained plagiarized passages and mannerisms. One, extraordinarily, earned me one of the school's annual prizes for essay writing, and it seemed only appropriate to choose one of Jefferies' books. I was intrigued by the idea of The Story of My Heart, *thinking it to be a piece of village patriotism of the kind written by C. Henry Warren, so I asked for that. Unfortunately none of the masters responsible for the prizes had ever heard of Jefferies and, assuming from the book's title that I'd ordered a piece of cheap romantic fiction, vetoed my choice until it had been thoroughly investigated.*

Richard Jefferies

First published as the introduction to *Landscapes with Figures:
An anthology of Richard Jefferies' prose*, Penguin, 1983

It is now nearly a century since Jefferies' death, yet it is still hard to say exactly what kind of writer he was. On the strength of the few of his books that are still widely read – *The Gamekeeper at Home, Nature Near London, Wildlife in a Southern County* – he is recognized as probably the most imaginative observer of the natural world of his century. More generally he is regarded as a 'country' writer, and that will certainly do as a rough description of his working territory. But in any less literal sense it is a definition which immediately begs the most important question about his work, for there is nothing conventionally rural about Jefferies. He was never a land-worker and for a good deal of his career did not even live in the countryside. His writing rarely has the qualities of peace and timelessness that are supposed to characterize 'rustic' literature. He can appear, sometimes inside a single piece of writing, as a small-town journalist, a romantic radical, a social historian and an apologist for the landowning class. The closer he is read the more the major concern of his work appears to be an implicit questioning of what a 'country writer' is, an exploration of the relationships that are possible between a reflective outsider, marginal in all senses to the real business of the land, and the hard imperatives of life in the fields. To what extent is 'the countryside' not just a fact of geography and a place of work but an emblem for a whole range of social and spiritual values? And if it has such intangible assets, who are the rightful inheritors?

As 'outsiders' urgently searching for a meaningful relationship with the land ourselves, Jefferies is very much our contemporary. Yet his life has repeatedly been mythologized. In the most telling version – out of the Golden Age by the Romantics – chance brings together this visionary spirit, born of ancient English farming stock, and the last remnants of an unblemished and untroubled countryside. The reality was rather different. Jefferies was raised on an unsuccessful small-holding in a county where, just twenty years before, labourers had fought pitched battles with the yeoman farmers. He began writing during the great agricultural depression of the 1870s, and died, after years of suffering from tuberculosis, when he was only 38.

We have to remember this history when reading Jefferies. But equally I believe, we have to remember the myths. A feature of his writing – moving as it does from its own brand of pastoral fantasy to exact social and natural descriptions – is the way it exposes our own tendency to simplify and glamorize rural life.

The sheer range of his output was formidable. In a working life of not much more than fifteen years he published nine novels and ten volumes of non-fiction. Another ten collections appeared posthumously. His non-fiction works were mostly quarried from more than four hundred essays and articles he contributed to some thirty different publications, from *The Livestock Journal* to the *Pall Mall Gazette*. He would write with equal willingness (though not always equal facility) technical pieces for the farming press, improving articles for home encyclopedias, and propaganda for Tory journals. In the high-circulation tabloids he pioneered the 'country diary', and the distinctive, discursive style he developed is still echoed in a score of local newspapers. In almost the same breath, it seems, he was able to retreat into mystical reveries of the kind typified by *The Story of My Heart*, and then burst into radical sermonizing. Partly he wrote as any freelance will – what he was paid to write by his editors; yet the shifts also happened unprompted, as Jefferies revised yet again his opinion of where he belonged in the rural scheme of things.

Although Jefferies' willingness to change his mind has sometimes been used as a reason for dismissing his work as trivial or untrustworthy, it can be refreshing to find this kind of flexibility in 'country' writing. For a *motif* that is so important in English literature, the countryside has been portrayed from a notoriously narrow set of views, and only exceptionally by those who worked on it themselves. Permanence and peace, consequently, have been sighted more often than change and conflict, and natural harmony (though this is often illusory too) taken to include social harmony. At worst, the indigenous human has been absorbed completely into the natural landscape as another kind of contented ruminant. This is a damaging process, and as Raymond Williams has pointed out, 'A fault can then occur in the whole ordering of the mind. Defence of a "vanishing Countryside" . . . can become deeply confused with that defence of the old rural order which is in any case being expressed by the landlords, the rentiers, and their literary sympathizers.'*

Although a long history of pastoral naïvety has understandably produced a widespread suspicion of onlookers' and outsiders' versions of the rural experience, this can lead in turn to another kind of bias, in which all such views are dismissed as aesthetic indulgences. Yet the cycles of birth, death, harvest and renewal which characterize the agricultural and natural worlds have been a powerful source of symbols at every level in our culture, even for those who do not live close to them. And there is a sense in which a settled rural landscape, whose

* *The Country and the City*, Chatto & Windus, 1973.

pattern of fields, farms and churches embodies the history of a hundred generations, *is* a vision of Eden, no matter what temptation and toil lie hidden behind it.

There has been no shortage of writers willing to ignore this problem of perspective and depict the countryside in simple black or white terms. Jefferies' accomplishment was to portray it in all shades with an equal vehemence and within the compass of a single working life. Although in the short term his versatility can look like shallowness or opportunism, in the context of his whole work it seems more like a rare kind of honesty, a genuine working through a problem which is increasingly familiar today.

The central character in what Jefferies once called 'The Field-Play' is the land-worker himself. The shift in the way he is depicted – from laggard to victim to hero – is the most striking expression of the movement of Jefferies' thinking. Even his physical characteristics are viewed in different ways. In the early 1870s he is described as a rather badly designed machine. Ten years later he is being explicitly compared to the form of a classical sculpture.

Typically, it was with a shrewd, unflattering sketch of the Wiltshire labourer that Jefferies pushed his writing before a national audience in 1872. The Agricultural Labourers' Union had been formed just two years earlier and there was mounting concern amongst landowners about its likely impact on the farm. Jefferies was working on the *North Wilts Herald* at the time, and realized that he was well placed to make an entry into the debate. He had a lifetime's experience of observing agricultural affairs, an adaptable and persuasive style, and enough ambition not to be averse to saying what his readers wanted to hear. So he composed the first of his now celebrated letters to *The Times* on the life and habits of the Wiltshire labourer and, in particular, on his uncouthness, laziness and more than adequate wages. It was by any standards a callous piece, written with apparent objectivity, but in fact with a calculated disdain that at times reduces the worker to little more than a beast of burden:

As a man, he is usually strongly built, broad-shouldered, and massive in frame, but his appearance is spoilt by the clumsiness of his walk and want of grace in his movements. . . . The labourer's muscle is that of a cart-horse, his motions lumbering and slow. His style of walk is caused by following the plough in early childhood, when the weak limbs find it is a hard labour to pull the heavy nailed boots from the thick clay soil. Ever afterwards he walks as if it were an exertion to lift his legs.

Jefferies was wearing his contempt on his sleeve, of course; but when he returned to the subject in the *Manchester Guardian* thirteen years later, it is hard to credit that it is the same man writing. Even the title of the piece (like those of many of his later essays) has a new subtlety, being less a description of what was to come than a frame of reference within which to read it: 'One of the New Voters' had little to do with voting or party loyalties but a great deal, implicitly, with the human right to the franchise. It recounted with meticulous detail and controlled anger a day in the life of Roger the reaper. Although he is still an abstraction, not a person, Roger is an altogether more real and sympathetic character than his predecessors. No longer an intemperate idler, but a man tied to long hours of dispiriting work without the capital or political power to find a way out, he none the less keeps his own private culture intact. Jefferies describes a scene in a pub after the day's work is over:

You can smell the tobacco and see the ale; you cannot see the indefinite power which holds men there – the magnetism of company and conversation. *Their* conversation, not *your* conversation; not the last book, the last play; not saloon conversation; but theirs – talk in which neither you nor any one of your condition could really join. To us there would seem nothing at all in that conversation, vapid and subjectless; to them it means much. We have not been through the same circumstances: our day has been differently spent, and the same words have therefore a varying value. Certain it is, that it is conversation that takes men to the public house. Had Roger been a horse he would have hastened to borrow some food, and having eaten that, would have cast himself at once upon his bed. Not being an animal, though his life and work were animal, he went with his friends to talk.

This was a remarkable recognition from a man who just a few years earlier had seen nothing but vacant faces amongst the labouring class. But what really lifts this essay above the level of ephemeral social comment is that Jefferies sets it in the context of the great drama of the harvest, in which toil, sunshine, beer and butterflies, cornfield weeds and the staff of life, are mixed together in perplexing contradiction:

The golden harvest is the first scene; the golden wheat, glorious under the summer sun. Bright poppies flower in its depths, and convolvulus climbs the stalks. Butterflies float slowly over the yellow surface as they might over a lake of colour. To linger by it, to visit it day by day, even to watch the sunset by it, and see it pale under the changing light, is a delight to the thoughtful mind. There is so much in the wheat, there are books of meditation in it, it is dear to the heart. Behind these beautiful aspects comes the reality of human labour – hours upon hours of heat and strain; there comes the reality of a rude life, and in the end little enough of gain. The wheat is beautiful, but human life is labour.

The central paradox of rural life has never been more plainly put. In another intense late essay, 'Walks in the Wheatfields' (1887), Jefferies likens the blinding, desperate gathering in of the harvest to 'gold fever . . . the whole village lived in the field . . . yet they seemed but a handful buried in the tunnels of a golden mine . . .'. The double meaning of 'living in' here is very forceful; at the start of the piece he compares the shape of a grain of wheat to an embryo or 'tiny man or woman . . . settled to slumber'. In the wheatfield, he suggests, 'transubstantiation is a fact . . .'

In his last years Jefferies was increasingly preoccupied with paradoxes that emerged when men lived close to nature. They seemed trapped in one way by their physical and biological needs, and in another by their sensibilities. If the ritual of harvest was paradoxical, so was all labour, which, depending on where you stood, could seem an act of nature or necessity, dignity or slavery. So, for that matter, was nature itself, which could be simultaneously cruel and beautiful. Jefferies' concern with these ambiguities was in part a reflection of his own uncertain social position, as a man who had devoted his life to the expression of rural life, but who had no real role in it himself. He found no solutions to this enigma; but as he explores some of its more practical ramifications – could villages be centres of social change as well as social stability, for instance? What were the respective rights of owners, workers and tourists over the land? – his mixed feelings of exclusion and concern come increasingly close to our modern worries about the countryside.

Richard Jefferies seemed destined to be a displaced person from childhood. He was born into a declining smallholding at Coate near Swindon in 1848. Although he was later to idealize both Coate and his father (who appears as the splendid, doomed figure of farmer Iden in the novel *Amaryllis at the Fair*, 1886) it does not seem to have been an especially happy household. A description of Coate in a letter from his father has a bitterness whose roots, one suspects, reach back to a time before Jefferies began upgrading his literary address to Coate Farm:

How could he think of describing Coate as such a pleasant place and deceive so I could not imagine, in fact nothing scarcely he mentions is in Coate proper only the proper one was not a pleasant one Snodeshill was the name on my Waggon and cart, he styled it Coate Farm it was not worthy of the name of Farm it was not Forty Acres of Land.*

When he was 4 years old Jefferies was sent away from Snodshill to live with his aunt in Sydenham. He stayed there for five years, visiting his parents for just one month's holiday a year. When he was 9 he returned home, but was quickly despatched to a succession of private schools in Swindon. Shunted about as if he were already a misfit, it is no wonder that he developed into a moody and solitary adolescent. He began reading Rabelais and the Greek Classics and spent long days roaming about Marlborough Forest. He had no taste for farm work and his father used to point with disgust to 'our Dick poking about in them hedges'. When he was 16 Jefferies ran away from home with his cousin, first to France and then to

* Cit. *Richard Jefferies: Man of the Fields*, ed. S. J. Looker and C. Porteous, John Baker 1965.

Liverpool, where he was found by the police and sent back to Swindon.

This habit of escape into fantasy or romantic adventure (it was later to become a characteristic of his fiction) must have been aggravated by the real-life decline of Coate. In 1865 the smallholding was badly hit by the cattle plague that was sweeping across southern England, and a short while later 14 acres had to be sold off. Jefferies had left school for good by this time, and in 1866 started work in Swindon on a new Conservative paper, the *North Wilts Herald*. He was employed as a jack-of-all-trades reporter and proof-reader, but seemed to spend a good deal of his time composing short stories for the paper. They were a collection of orthodox Victorian vignettes of thwarted love, murder and historical romance, mannered in tone and coloured by antiquarian and classical references. Although they are of no real literary value, they may have been useful to Jefferies as a way of testing and exercising his imaginative muscles.

The next few years brought further frustrations and more elaborate retreats. In 1868 he began to be vaguely ill and had to leave his job on the *Herald*. In 1870 he took a long recuperative holiday in Brussels. He was extravagantly delighted by the women, the fashions, the manners, the sophistication of it all, and from letters to his aunt it is clear what he was beginning to think of the philistinism of Wiltshire society.

But circumstances forced him to return there in 1871, and to a situation that must have seemed even less congenial than when he had left. With the farm collapsing around them his parents resented his idleness and irresponsibility. He had no job and no money. He was able to sell a few articles to his old newspaper, but they were not enough, and he had to pawn his gun. His life began to slip into an anxious, hand-to-mouth existence that had more in common with the stereotype of the urban freelance than with a supposed 'son of the soil'. He started novels, but was repeatedly diverted by a procession of psychosomatic illnesses. He wrote a play and a rather dull memoir on the family of his prospective Member of Parliament, Ambrose Goddard. The most unusual projects in this period were two pamphlets: *Reporting, Editing and Authorship:*

Practical Hints for Beginners, and *Jack Brass, Emperor of England.*
This was a right-wing broadsheet that ridiculed what Jefferies
saw as the dangers of populism: '. . . Educate! educate! educate! Teach every one to rely on their own judgement, so as to
destroy the faith in authority, and lead to a confidence in their
own reason, the surest method of seduction . . . .' It was a
heavy-handed satire, and though it may not have been intended very seriously, Jefferies was to remember it with
embarrassment in later years.

But by this stage he had already made a more substantial
political and literary debut with his letters to *The Times* on the
subject of the Wiltshire labourer. It is important to remember
the context in which these appeared. Agricultural problems of
one kind or another had been central issues in British politics
for much of the nineteenth century. But the land-workers
themselves had been given sparse attention, and though they
had been impoverished by the cumulative effects of farm
mechanization, wage and rent levels, and the appropriation of
the commonlands, their own protests had been sporadic and
ineffectual. Then in 1870 Joseph Arch and some of his fellow
workers gathered together illicitly in their Warwickshire village and formed the Agricultural Labourers' Union.

This was a new development in the countryside and raised
new anxieties amongst landowners. The rioting and rick-
burning of the 1820s had fitted into a familiar stereotype of
peasant behaviour and had been comparatively easily contained. But organization was a different matter, seeming to
introduce an ominously urban challenge to the rural order
and, by implication, to the social fabric of the nation which
rested on it.

Jefferies' hybrid background may have helped him understand these worries better than most, and it was the sense of
moral affront sounded in his letters that won him sympathy
from the landowning classes. The correspondence became the
subject of an editorial in *The Times,* and Jefferies was soon
offered more journalistic work in the same vein. Over the next
few years he wrote copiously on rural and agricultural affairs
for journals such as *Fraser's Magazine* and *The Livestock Journal.*
Collectively these pieces are more informed and compassion-

ate than *The Times'* letters. Jefferies sympathized with the sufferings of the labourers and their families, but believed that many of their habitual responses to trouble – particularly their reluctance to accept responsibility for their own fate – simply made matters worse. Wage demands alienated the farmers, who were their natural patrons and allies. Drink led to the kind of family break-ups described in 'John Smith's Shanty' (1874). The only certain remedies were hard work and self-discipline.

This has been a perennial theme in Conservative philosophy and there are times when Jefferies' recommendations have a decidedly modern ring, as, for instance, in 'The Labourer's Daily Life' (1874): 'The sense of home ownership engenders a pride in the place, and all his better feelings are called into play.' Yet even at this early stage, Jefferies' conservatism has a liberal edge, and anticipates the libertarian, self-help politics of his later years. He speaks out in favour of allotments, libraries, cottage hospitals, women's institutes and other mutual associations as means towards parish independence. And he begins to suggest that the farm and the village – the basic units of rural life – owed their survival and strength not so much to some immemorial order but precisely to their capacity to incorporate change and new ideas into a well-tried framework.

The increasing amount of work Jefferies was doing for London-based journals encouraged him to move to Surbiton in 1877, when he was 28 years of age. Rather to his surprise he enjoyed London, discovering in it not only many unexpectedly green corners, but an exciting quality of movement and vivacity. As Claude Monet was to do in his paintings of Leicester Square and Westminster Bridge, Jefferies saw the rush of traffic and the play of streetlights almost as if they were natural events. In 'The Lions in Trafalgar Square' (1892) even the people are absorbed:

At summer noontide, when the day surrounds us and it is bright light even in the shadow, I like to stand by one of the lions and yield to the old feeling. The sunshine glows on the dusky creature, as it seems, not on the surface but under the skin, as if it came up from out of the limb. The roar of the rolling wheels sinks and becomes distant as the sound of a waterfall when dreams are coming. All abundant life is smoothed and levelled, the abruptness of the individuals lost in the flowing current like separate flowers drawn along in a border, like music heard so far off that the notes are molten and the theme only remains.

'Lions', like most of the London essays, was written during a later phase of Jefferies' life. Perhaps because of his uncertainty about his own social role, he rarely wrote about his current circumstances, but about what he had just left behind. In Swindon much of his work was concerned with the fantasy world of his adolescence. In Surbiton he is remembering his life at Coate, albeit in a rather idealized form.

The pieces that were to make up his first fully-fledged non-fiction work, *The Gamekeeper at Home,* were amongst these reminiscences, and were initially published in serial form in the *Pall Mall Gazette* between December 1877 and spring 1878. It is of some significance that Jefferies chose as his subjects 'the master's man' and the practical business of policing a sporting estate. The game laws were a crucial instrument for expressing and maintaining the class structure of the nineteenth-century countryside. Although poaching was an economic necessity for many families, it was also an act of defiance against the presumptions of landowners. They, for their part, often viewed the taking of wild animals from their land as a more fundamental breach of their 'natural' rights than outright stealing.

Jefferies doesn't challenge this assumption in *The Gamekeeper at Home.* In a chapter on the keeper's enemies, for instance, he moves smoothly from weasels, stoats and magpies to 'semi-bohemian trespassers', boys picking sloes and old women gathering firewood: '. . . how is the keeper to be certain,' he argues, 'that if the opportunity were offered these gentry would not pounce upon a rabbit or anything else?'

This strand in Jefferies' writing reaches a culmination in *Hodge and his Masters.* This collection of portraits of the rural middle class – speculators, solicitors, landowners, parsons – was serialized in the London *Standard* between 1878 and 1880. Its hero is the self-made, diligent yeoman farmer. If he should fail it is because he has become lazy or drunk, or has forgotten his place in society:

There used to be a certain tacit agreement among all men that those who possessed capital, rank or reputation should be treated with courtesy. That courtesy did not imply that the landowner, the capitalist, or the minister of religion, was necessarily himself superior. But it did imply that those who administered property really represented the general order in which all were interested . . . . These two characteristics, moral apathy and contempt of property – i.e. of social order – are probably exercising considerable influence in shaping the labourer's future.

Jefferies grows shriller as he outlines the agents of these malign forces – poachers, publicans, the unemployed, the dispossessed and dependent. Hodge himself, the ordinary labourer, remains invisible, except when Jefferies is rebuking him, in now familiar style, for his greed, bad cooking, lack of culture and laziness. How lucky he is, Jefferies remarks, to work only in the hours of daylight. After this, it is hard to take seriously the book's closing note of regret about the insulting charity of the workhouse.

Yet alongside (and sometimes inside) these sour social commentaries he had begun writing short studies in natural history. They are lightly and sharply observed, and one senses Jefferies' relief at having an escape route from the troubled world of human affairs. *Wildlife in a Southern County* was serialized in the *Pall Mall Gazette* during 1878, and its contents give some indication of what a versatile writer he was. There are pieces on orchards, woods, rabbits, ants, stiles, the ague, and 'noises in the air'. The descriptions of the weather are especially convincing – perhaps because he saw this as one area which was beyond the corrupting influence of human society.

During this stage in his life his writing developed a characteristic discursiveness that was no doubt partly a result of his working as a jobbing journalist and having regularly to fill columns of a fixed length. Yet it was also a way of talking to his new non-rural audience. They are ramblings in an almost literal sense: anecdotes, observations, musings roll by as if Jefferies was addressing his companions on a walk.

In *Round About a Great Estate* (1880) this conversational style is used to great effect and helps make this the most unaffectedly charming of all Jefferies' books. It is an ingenuous, buoyant collection of parish gossip, of characters and events that seem to have been chanced upon by accident. Yet it is celebratory rather than nostalgic. Jefferies remarks in his preface to the original edition:

In this book some notes have been made of the former state of things before it passes away entirely. But I would not have it therefore thought that I wish it to continue or return. My sympathies and hopes are with the light of the future, only I should like it to come from nature. The clock should be read by the sunshine, not the sun timed by the clock.

The worst thing that can be said about these natural history and documentary essays is not that they are inconsequential, but that they are impersonal and generalized. Even at his most perceptive, Jefferies viewed natural life with the same kind of detachment as he regarded the labourer: it aroused his curiosity but rarely his sympathy. But at the beginning of the 1880s a new intimacy starts to appear in his writing. He allows us to share specific experiences and deeply personal feelings. He seems, at last, to be *engaged*. A set of pieces on the fortunes of a trout trapped in a London brook, for instance, show us Jefferies in a very unfamiliar light – concerned, sentimental, and increasingly aware of his own vulnerability.

There can be little doubt that one of the major influences on Jefferies during these years was his deteriorating health. The illness that was eventually to kill him began in earnest in 1881 and was diagnosed as a generalized tuberculosis. During 1882 he went to Brighton to recuperate, but he found only temporary relief, and signs of his pain and disenchantment are visible in almost all the remainder of his work.

Much of this period, perhaps predictably, was taken up with escapist novels. *Greene Ferne Farm* (1880) is an old-fashioned pastoral with a dialect-speaking Chorus. *Bevis* (1882), a book for children, is set in Jefferies' boyhood Wiltshire, which the young heroes transform into a fabulous playground for their fantasies. *After London* (1885) is a bitter vision of the collapse of urban civilization and of the city reclaimed by forest and swamp. Yet even with, so to speak, the slate wiped clean, Jefferies still chooses to create a woodland feudal society, complete with reconstituted poachers as savages. There is some fine descriptive writing in his fiction (particularly in *Amaryllis at the Fair*, which is based on an idealized version of his own family), yet as novels they can hardly be viewed as successes. They have no real movement, either in the development of the plot or of the individual characters. David Garnett described *Amaryllis* as 'a succession of stills, never a picture in motion', * and Jefferies himself declared he would have been happy to have seen it published as 'scenes of country life' rather than as a novel.

During the early eighties he was also working on his 'soul-life', a kind of spiritual autobiography that was published as *The Story of My Heart* in 1883. Like all mystical works this is comprehensible to the degree to which one shares the writer's faith – which in this case is an intense pantheism. Yet the book is an account of a meditation rather than a complete religion. (Some of the short, rhythmically written passages even read like mantras.) Typically, Jefferies goes to a 'thinking place' – a tree, a stream, or more often the sea – lies under the sun and prays that he may have a revelation. He wishes to transcend the flesh, to transcend nature itself, though he cannot express what he wants, nor what, if anything, he has found. 'The only idea I can give,' he writes, 'is that there is another idea.' Yet if the mystical sections of *The Story* are typified by this kind of wordplay – sincerely meant, no doubt, but meaningless – there is another strand of more earthly idealism in the book concerned with a belief in the perfectability of man and the degradation of labour, themes that were to become increasingly prominent in his work.

Although it is mostly impenetrable to a casual reader, the soul-searching of *The Story of My Heart* seemed to free Jefferies from many of his social and literary uncertainties. After 1883

* Introduction to *Amaryllis at the Fair*, Dent, 1939.

his writing has a new commitment and assurance of style. He accepts his outsider's role, and argues that a respect for, and intimacy with, nature and the land are of universal human importance. He worries, for instance, about trends in agricultural modernization and their likely implications for wildlife. He attacks the grubbing-out of hedgerows and the ploughing of old grassland. He defends the otter, and argues for the townsman's right of access to the countryside (see particularly 'The Modern Thames', 1884).

These were specific expressions of a deeper change in Jefferies' whole ideology. By the mid-eighties he had begun to argue for the extension of the franchise, and at times to go beyond the humane concern of 'One of the New Voters' to an out and out socialist position. In a remarkable late essay, 'Primrose Gold in our Villages' (1887), he describes how the new Conservative alliances in the countryside, which had once opposed the labourers' vote, were now moving in to appropriate it. 'Primrose Gold' is unlike anything he had written previously. It is sophisticated, witty, elliptical, and bitterly ironic. It also deals in allusion and metaphor, which are in short supply in his earlier, more literal writings. As Raymond Williams has remarked: "Primrose Gold": the phrase is so exact. The simple flower as a badge of political manoeuvre; the yellow of the flower and of the money that is the real source of power; the natural innocence, the political dominance: it is all there.'*

In his late essays Jefferies begins to write of the politics, history and landscape of the countryside as if they were aspects of a single experience. Although he would still turn in slight pieces on seaside beaches and song birds when it was required of him, he was beginning to suggest that nature was not something apart from use, but a world that we were part of and in which we might see reflected some of our own qualities as living creatures. In 'Out of Doors in February' (1882), for instance, he explains the optimism he saw in the images of winter, and in the living world's annual triumph over dark and cold:

* *The Country and the City*, Chatto & Windus, 1973.

The lark, the bird of the light, is there in the bitter short days. Put the lark then for winter, a sign of hope, a certainty of summer. Put, too, the sheathed buds there, on tree and bush, carefully wrapped around with the case that protects them as a cloak. Put, too, the sharp needles of the green corn . . . . One memory of the green corn, fresh beneath the sun and wind, will lift up the heart from the clods.

That was one kind of answer to the enigma of the toiler in the field: nature as a redemptive force that could smooth away the distortions of civilization. In 'Golden Brown' (1884) Jefferies writes enviously of the health and habits of the Kent fruit pickers and of 'the life above this life to be obtained from the constant presence with the sunlight and the stars'.

Yet at no time had he believed that complete human fulfilment could be achieved by a simple surrender to natural (or artificially rustic) rhythms. In an odd and not always rational way he also believed in that specifically human concept, progress. As early as 1880 he had declared that his sympathies and hopes were with 'the light of the future'. He wanted, in Edwards Thomas's wonderfully exact phrase, 'the light railway to call at the farmyard gate'.*

But for Jefferies himself neither nature nor progress could any longer provide a release. He spent 1887, the last year of his life, as an invalid in Goring, in pain and poverty. His view of the world was confined to what he could glimpse through a window, and his thoughts by that paradox that had haunted him, in one form or another, for most of his life. He had dreamed of men living with the easy grace of birds in flight, yet realized that the self-awareness that made that ambition possible would prevent it ever being fulfilled. In 'Hours of Spring' he writes mournfully of 'the old, old error: I love the earth and therefore the earth loves me.' Man was in the unique and probably unenviable position of being both part of nature and a conscious interpreter of it. Hence the crises of perspective that affected young political commentator and nostalgic old man-of-the-fields alike.

These last essays, particularly 'Walks in the Wheatfields'

* *Richard Jefferies*, 1909; Faber edition 1978.

and 'My Old Village', are poignant and embittered, but written with great power and clarity. In the end – inevitably perhaps – he returns to introversion and, in 'Nature and Books', for example, rejects both naturalistic and scientific analysis of the colour of flowers: 'I want the inner meaning and the understanding of wild flowers in the meadow. . . . Why are they? What end? What purpose?' For Jefferies, these questions were almost metaphysical! But they have not lost their relevance, and we ask them more urgently now, knowing, like Jefferies, that the partial answers of landowners and scientists alike are not sufficient.

The idealization of country life that characterized much of Richard Jefferies' early prose has become an increasingly prominent note in writing about the countryside. In the 1970s it swelled to a clamour, and books on herbs, wholefoods, bird-spotting and self-sufficiency began to dominate the best-sellers' charts. This was in part a reflection of a genuine change in public attitudes towards the environment. But many people found rusticity more romantic at a distance (preferably in the past), and for them the printed tokens were sufficient in themselves. Amongst these nothing rivalled the success, or the blandness, of just one title published in 1977 – The Country Diary of an Edwardian Lady. By 1980 2¼ million copies had been sold, and an industry with a cumulative revenue of £13 million had grown up to market Country Diary cards, teacloths, and seed collections. As one publisher brazenly put it in advertisements for his own contributions to the bandwagon: 'Nostalgia: the past with a profitable future.'*

The following review of The Country Diary was published before the full extent of its impact had become clear, and despite its brevity I've included it here because I believe it was the only 'serious' notice written at the time. As subsequent events made clear, it might have been more appropriate to review the publishing attitudes that promoted this book and its myriads of imitators. This has since been excellently done by Fraser Harrison in an essay entitled 'Corrupt Grief' in his book Strange Land.† His view of nostalgia as a distorted and exploitable expression of real and deeply felt losses connects with many of the themes in this present book. 'Nostalgia,' he writes, 'can hardly keep pace with the demand for any corner of peace and companionship, any little walled garden of the imagination.'

* Since I wrote this, Country Diary armchairs have come on the market, and stage musical and TV soap opera versions are under production.
† Sidgwick & Jackson, 1982.

The Country Diary

First published in *The Times*, 16 June 1977

In the spring of 1920 Edith Holden, a Warwickshire lady in her 49th year and an illustrator by profession, fell into the Thames whilst picking chestnut buds at Kew, and drowned. Of the many poignant features associated with her early death, not the least is the possibility that, had she lived out her natural span, she might well have thrown away her personal note-books, one of which has now been published as *The Country Diary of an Edwardian Lady*.

It is always discomforting to read a diary that was plainly never meant for public eyes, though in this case it is not from any sense of prying. There are no skeletons laid bare in this parish record, no secret passions revealed, no savour of the age, or even, sadly, of the writer herself. It is simply not that kind of book, and never set out to be. Edith Holden's journal for 1906 is a simple account of birds arriving and flowers opening, handwritten with a fastidious pen, illustrated by the author's own watercolour sketches, and adorned here and there with favourite snatches of verse. It is painstaking, pretty and utterly banal. It has something of the quality of a child's scrapbook, kept to while away the evenings and entertain family and friends. Yet here it is, pushed into the limelight amidst a great deal of trumpeting, and poor Edith Holden must be judged as the diarist and naturalist she never pre-tended to be.

The best things in it are her paintings of flowers (her birds are an embarrassment) – but then they should be, since it was from these that she earned most of her livelihood. They are accurate for the most part, and have a slight, dry-summer warmth. But in case anyone should think this exceptional in an Edwardian woman, remember that Anne Pratt's four-volume

151

Flowering Plants had been out for more than fifty years, and contained not only hundreds of her own paintings, but a text that whilst reading a little crankily today, was adventurous, sceptical and inquisitive.

From the evidence of this book at least, Edith Holden had none of these qualities. She saw what one was seasonally expected to see, noted it, and moved one. 'March 1: March has come in like a lamb with a warm wind and rain from the south-west . . . . 4: Glorious sunshine. First warm day of spring. All the skylarks up and singing in the blue . . . . 6th: Tonight a toad was discovered jumping in the hall; it must have come in through the garden door which had been standing open all day.' And so it goes on, the excitement real enough, I'm sure, but usually borrowed, always on cue and never escaping through the stilted language. There is scarcely a fresh or original insight in the whole year. 'July 7: In a cornfield of growing wheat, I saw a number of blossoms of the Opium poppy. Their large red and purple blooms made fine patches of colour among the green blades.' Opium in the wheat? A toad in the hall? Did her curiosity really stop at these bare entries?

The book's appeal stems in part from being rooted in a period when it was still possible to be care-free about the countryside. But I suspect that its construction had a lot in common with the sampler, a formal exercise for private consumption. To have made it public as it stands not only misrepresents what was an advanced and popular form before the days of typewriter and snapshot albums; but also, I would guess, Edith Holden herself, who I'm sure was a more interesting Edwardian lady than suggested by this happenstance record.

A Mushroom Grew in Berkeley Square

First published in *Punch*, 20 October 1976

In the days when Radio 4 was still the Home Service, one of the favourite questions to the panels on quiz shows was 'What would you try hardest to save if your house was burning down?' To judge from the swelling flood of books on growing vegetables in used car tyres and putting up a windmill on the top of the flowering cherry, the problem has been revived with a thoroughly modern twist: what should you try to hoard against the eventual breakdown of civilization as we know it? Corrugated iron for a solar roof? A sack of high-protein beans? Or a certificate in butchering? The most all-embracing of the compendiums so far published, *The Survival Handbook: self-sufficiency for everyone*, by Michael Allaby (Macmillan), tells you how to slaughter and dress a goat in one succinct paragraph and, as a bonus, how to deliver a child and cope with 'commune neurosis' (half a page each).

It is sad that so many of these guides are pervaded by this air of a self-congratulatory game of consequences, for the anxieties which have produced them are real and urgent enough. No one could seriously doubt any longer that industrial society is profligate in its squandering of raw materials and its stunting of human resources. If it doesn't finally bury itself under a pall of unrecycled junk it will likely split apart from sheer frustration. And whether you decide to drop out now or wait for the worst, the remedy seems to be the same: we need to live in smaller, more intimate human groups and in a less destructive relationship with nature.

The problem is that few of these books seem to have worked out whether they are practical instruction manuals for improving the quality of life now, or pocket scenarios for a post-apocalyptic world. One small quibble, for instance, concerns the way that badgers are treated. Many self-sufficiency books

153

give recipes for badger hams, notwithstanding the fact that with another hat on ecologists are campaigning for the legal protection of this much persecuted animal. (Realistic compromises are possible: one frugal Dorset woman I met recently had found a dead badger on the road, skinned it herself, used the pelt as a doormat, rendered the fat down for the tits, and fed the meat – at which her over-civilized dogs turned up their noses – to an orphaned owlet. But then she had all the advantages of a late-industrial country cottage, complete with electric cooker.)

At the moment real self-sufficiency is only an option for the landed élite. Even John Seymour, whose informative and convincing *Self-Sufficiency** was the forerunner of the whole cult, has admitted that without 60 acres of Welsh farmland and a private income from writing and broadcasting (and you can't get much further into high technology than that), he would have found the exercise impossible. Uncompromised millennial outposts are just not possible in a tight-knit society like ours, even as experiments. As the BBC is discovering, even a replica Iron Age village needs to satisfy the fire regulations.

But coping with compromise doesn't have the spartan thrill of Utopian daydreaming. So the natural longings of the rest of us (whose patch is more likely to be a 50-square-foot backyard) are ignored, and we are abandoned to official inanities like 'taking a bath with a friend'.

Working an allotment is anything but a frivolous contribution, yet Michael Leapman's (*The Times'* Diarist) engaging account of his first year on a plot behind Brixton prison (*One Man and his Plot†*) is a shade too flippant about monster Marmande tomatoes and the fashionable aspects of growing your own food – more *The Good Life* than *The Survivors*. I can understand the dangers to him of being seen with the wrong trends, but plants are at the productive heart of things, and deserve more respect. The two most exciting and original alternative technology books to come out this year both have plants as their heroes, as supreme models of self-sufficiency in

* Faber & Faber, 1973.
† John Murray, 1976.

their own right. *Nature, Mother of Invention,* * by Felix Paturi, urges us to look at the devices plants use to solve their own technological problems, and which they have necessarily evolved by adapting to their environment rather than trying to subdue it. I hope every water authority thirsty to bulldoze new reservoirs will read the chapter on plant hydraulics. Desert cacti, for instance, gather water by nothing more energy-consuming than the topography of their spines, which, like a comb drawn through the hair, attract electrically charged water particles from the air.

Forest Farming†, by Douglas and Hart, is about an ancient idea which is just being rediscovered – the principle of continuous yield. Only a few weeks ago we were told of one extraordinary example of this, the possibility that forty barrels of petrol per acre could be extracted each year from a shrubby relative of our garden spurges.

But most back-to-nature addicts are more interested in rosemary shampoo than vegetable petroleum. Books on herbs, those living manifestations of all the qualities seemingly lacking from a culture based on mass production, abound: herbs for footbaths and linen cupboards, herbs for curing sick chickens and casseroling healthy ones. Mrs M. Grieve's classic *A Modern Herbal*, just reissued by Penguin, is a fascinating encyclopedia of herbal fact and fiction. Unfortunately the good lady doesn't discriminate between the two, and there is much magical nonsense in the book (knobbly roots for piles, etc.). So it is a relief that there is at last a book which catalogues those European herbs which have passed the efficacy tests of conventional medicine: *Medicinal Plants*,‡ by Hans Fluck. In global terms, they make up a huge company: over 50 per cent of prescriptions still contain a plant-based ingredient. Yet in spite of the increasing dangers of synthetic chemicals, we have only screened 4 per cent of the world's plants for effective drugs.

But I have a feeling that even the most reputable books are used more for fireside rehearsals than as field manuals. And it can't be long before the ultimate escapist read, some *Supersur-*

* Thames and Hudson, 1976.
† Watkins Publishing, 1976.
‡ Foulsham, 1976.

vivor's Yearbook, appears. Though, come to think of it, it could well, with tongue in chic, tell you how to build a solar oven in a bed-sit – which is just the note that is lacking from almost all these books.

PART FIVE

'...In a Green Shade'

Vole *has been mentioned in credits a number of times already, and since it is now an extinct species, it merits an explanatory note, and perhaps even an epitaph. The idea was Richard Boston's, and he called a number of us together in the autumn of 1976, with a view to starting a new journal. There were by this time any number of enviromentally conscious (and some environmentally self-conscious) magazines, but we felt that none of them quite caught either the needs of the moment or the mood of the growing green movement. The straightforwardly ecological were heavy, doctrinaire, and barely readable. The more traditional country journals were frequently frivolous, naïve and either apolitical or deeply conservative. None of them appeared to have the slightest sense of humour.* Vole, *we hoped, would be radical but nonaligned, ecologically informed but able to hold its head alongside the literary monthlies (the media having largely forgotten that nature was part of our culture), and never becoming sombre at any price. The working title was 'The Questing Vole', inspired by Evelyn Waugh's satirical novel on the press,* Scoop. *(Its hero, you may remember, wrote a country column called 'Lush Places', whose most memorable sentence was 'Feather-footed through the plashy fen passes the questing vole'.) It was shortened to* Vole *by the time the first issue came out in the summer of 1977, but the small mammal which Posy Simmonds drew for our logo — pencil behind ear, digit raised in admonition — was still undeniably questing. It was also undeniably small, comic and querulous.*

Vole *prospered for a couple of years and survived for two more, and in its own small way became a bit of an institution. Some measure of its reputation and range can be seen from its regular list of contributors: Richard Adams, Miles Kington, John Fowles, Richard North and E. P. Thompson, for example. Less frequently John Arlott wrote on cricket, Jeremy Sandford on Kilvert and Jonathan Raban on the Thames.*

Vole *succumbed in the summer of 1981 to a combination of the usual ills that plague small magazines – and perhaps to the fact that it was becoming increasingly hard to raise a smile about our chosen subjects. The magazine never lost its gingery edge, but the later issues lacked the idiosyncratic flair of the earlier. It is hard now to think of any other national magazine which would be able to accommodate the kind of material that went into the first score of issues.*

The following pieces include three examples from a countryside column I wrote, whose title, taken from Andrew Marvell's poem, 'The Garden', I've borrowed in turn as the title for this book. By contrast, there is also a much longer piece on the BBC's Iron Age Farm project.

Summer 1977 (trial issue)

Back in the mid-sixties the science fiction writer J. G. Ballard published a story about 'bioplastic' clothes (their 'living tissues were still growing, softly adapting themselves to the contours of her body, repairing themselves as the fibres became worn or grimy. Upstairs in her wardrobe the gowns and dresses purred on their hangers like the drowsing inmates of some arboreal zoo'). The Ipswich seed merchants, Thompson and Morgan, haven't quite perfected the patent on these yet, but if you want to keep up with the only marginally less exotic innovations of our green revolution, there is nothing to beat their annual catalogue, whose contents (and prose) are a match for Ballard at his most exuberant. It is a manual of organic gardening, a futurist cookbook and a guide to all manner of plants, old, new and frankly experimental.

During recent years T and M have introduced to Britain grow-your-own soya beans and the first commercial range of hydroponic sprouting seeds. In 1976 they began despatching 8,000-strong honey bee colonies to 'your nearest passenger station' for a mere £30. This year's innovations include green manure, half a dozen Chinese vegetables (plus a Wok to cook them in) and a vegetable bath sponge (the skeleton of the gourd *Luffa cylindrica*). If your herbaceous beds are already festooned with these the catalogue can still help. Did it occur to you that the surplus could be used for stuffing mattresses?

They have dropped tubs of horse mushrooms (as well as the

bees) in favour of pre-spawned logs of Shii-take toadstools, currently attracting interest because of their anti-viral properties, and whose flavour T and M describe as 'reminiscent of an exotic blend of filet mignon and lobster'. And gourmets with a taste for other kinds of scavenging organisms will be pleased they have added an offer of fifty live carp to stock a garden stew-pond. I cannot begin to grasp the delivery problems on this one. And what will the Post Office make of parcels of fully-hatched *Encarsia formosa* (£8.25 a packet), an alien weevil which controls greenhouse white fly by laying its eggs in their larvae?

No one is likely to forget the summer of 76. It was the year tropical yuccas bloomed in back gardens, and the *Sun* ran a pin-up of a runaway gourd whose pendulous fruits had to be supported in pairs of tights.

Two more modest, but equally significant plants which sprouted here, courtesy of the sun, were on show just before Christmas at the annual exhibition of the Botanical Society. This was held in the Herbarium Room of the Natural History Museum in London, and so much did the inscrutable wall-to-ceiling cabinets dwarf the exhibition tables, that I almost missed the evidence for the best-kept botanical secret of the year. It was a photograph of a species of mirror orchid, previously known only from the Mediterranean, which last summer bloomed on a stretch of downland in southern England. It is a striking flower, related to our own bee orchid, but with a brilliant blue reflective patch on its lower lip. The problem is how it suddenly succeeded in extending its range by more than 700 miles. It may have been planted (there is apparently a rogue orchid fancier in the area) but orchids are notoriously difficult to introduce to the wild. And given the fact that many of our native orchids bloomed far north of their usual stations last summer, it is just possible that it was a genuine wild sprouting, from wind-blown or dormant seed.

The other surprise, also an aberrant sprouting, was a neatly mounted sesame plant, found in Cambridge Sewage Works in September. Sesame is native in the Eastern tropics, but its seeds are used a good deal in Asian cooking (and on hamburger buns) in the West. The plants (there were two) were growing amidst a multitude of fruiting tomatoes, soya beans and water-melons – all this just a few miles from the meadows of Grantchester. What is happening at High Table? Have the Arabs bought King's College? And what kind of digestive system sends whole, fertile soya beans to the sludge beds?

There were all kinds of weather on the Suffolk coast at New Year: frosted marshes, spring rain, African sunsets. Everything, in fact, except real arctic weather and arctic birds. Down in Gloucestershire a group of Siberian white-fronted geese that had arrived early, supposedly fleeing from bad weather, had flown right into it – showing up yet again the nonsense about animals' prowess at long-range weather forecasting.

In Suffolk the only goose I saw on New Year's Day was a solitary brent, normally the most gregarious of all. As the sun set and the local farmers came out for their evening walks with shotgun and dog, it flew up anxiously towards the west – alone, conspicuous and too low for safety. I was glad that it had vanished in the gloom by the time a gun went off approximately in the direction it had flown. The main thing I have against wildfowling – which, in these conditions, seems to me the least obnoxious of blood sports – is the way it brutalizes our relationship with birds. It is a leveller of the worst sort, punishing the lonely and the hungry, reducing living birds not just to dead flesh but to nondescript members of a species. Flying free, they are enjoyed in common; snatched out of the sky, they are turned into private possessions.

October 1977

I have a Victorian bird book which includes a succinct account of the one and only visit ever made to this country by the Caribbean capped petrel: 'A Capped petrel was once found by a boy in a furze bush near Swaffham; it bit his hand, and he thereupon killed it, and made it into a British bird.' We are a bit less crude in our methods now, but I fear that old imperialist spirit is by no means dead in natural history circles. The September issue of *British Birds* carries a blow-by-blow account of how a Siberian blue robin, on its first recorded visit to Europe, was 'made into a British bird'. This little vagrant, blown off its usual migration route by a massive anticyclone over the Baltic in late October 1975, had put down in the Channel Islands – or more precisely into one of the mist-nets which are strung around our coasts during the autumn migration. This is how its captors described their find: 'Hanging in the net was a small passerine and, as he extracted it, PJG realized that the species was unknown to him.' Having 'safely bagged the bird', as they disconcertingly put it, they go on to weigh it, measure it, and calibrate every one of its major wing feathers. The bird 'remained silent during handling and we were hopeful of studying it in the field. Unfortunately, upon release it flew off immediately, calling "tchak" as it did so.' 'Tchak' is the nearest a robin can get to screaming, which this unfortunate individual, 4,000 miles off-track, tired, hungry, terrified, hung up by its feet in a net for God knows how many hours, no doubt very much wanted to do.

I am probably being oversentimental. I am sure that the bird was treated with care and affection and according to the strict rules which govern authorized scientific netting. But I am bothered about the attitudes towards birds of supposed bird lovers who desire, for the most dubious of reasons, to trap

163

birds at the moment of their greatest exhaustion and insecurity, and then to process them as if they were so many pieces of baggage. Some trapping and ringing – of seabirds, for instance – has yielded important knowledge about oceanic pollution. But it seems to me inexcusably degrading to both birds and handlers when the outcome is likely to be nothing more than another species on the 'British List'.

But at least the robin escaped with its life, which is more than can be said for the clutch of bearded tits destroyed by a gang of birders who invaded Radipole Lake in Dorset this summer, and began flinging lumps of concrete into the reedbeds to flush a male little bittern which had been seen there. There has been a depressing number of such incidents in recent years. When bird-watching becomes nothing more than a cover for atavistic cravings to tame and catalogue, to *possess*, then I think it would be more honestly done with a gun again. And if it lacks any kind of respect for or delight in the birds themselves, does rarity-chasing begin to turn 'nature into a kind of golf-course where you go to amuse yourself at weekends; into the mirror in which you flaunt your skill at naming'? That was John Fowles's description of what he called the 'hobbyist's' approach to nature: 'It drains nature of its complexity, of its richness, of its poetries, of its symbolism and correspondences, of its power to arouse emotion – of all its potential centrality in human existence.'

Yet, done with a sense of humour and affection, I can't see too much harm in the deliberate hunt for new 'meetings'. John Gooders – ornithology's Michelin – once described how novice birders could break the 200-species barrier in one year flat. For those with tolerant employers and a rally driver's stamina ('Drive up after work and spend the night near Shap Fell') there could scarcely be a more invigorating way of becoming acquainted both with birds and the British landscape.

I must confess at this stage to having my own list, rather discreditably marked up in faint and untidy pencil, as if I was trying to persuade myself they were just notes, not a tally at all. Yet, looking through it, I am struck at how much it encapsulates the meanings which birds hold for me. First encounters can be strong meat, and can irrevocably connect a bird in your mind with a particular landscape, a time of year, even a moment in your own life. My first redstart was the first bird I saw in close-up through my first pair of second-hand binoculars. (I'd been given them as a prize for passing the 11-plus.) I was transfixed when what I thought were robins darting up and down from a thick hillside hedge suddenly developed, through the lenses, swaggering chestnut tails. My first, and only, corncrake rasped out its song in an otherwise utterly silent Irish hay meadow, still twilit at midnight – though only after it had been stirred by the sound of 'a penknife being scraped against the bumper of our car. My first black-tailed godwits I saw because my first Montagu's harrier put them up from the Norfolk coastal marshes where they were nesting for the first time since the early nineteenth century. The two pairs of godwits went for this huge bird of prey (now Britain's rarest) like kamikaze pilots. They towered up vertically from the marsh in a V-formation, straight at the bewildered harrier, which can rarely have been harassed by such remorseless and well-drilled mobbers. They looped round it, dived at it, rose up at it in waves, never breaking that tight arrow formation. To see such rare and exquisite birds by themselves would have been a privilege; to witness the crossing of their paths as the godwits fought to re-establish themselves on their old breeding site was probably the experience of a lifetime, and mightily rich in 'symbolism and correspondences'.

But that stretch of marshland along the north Norfolk coast (now almost completely protected for its whole 40 miles) has always been a paradise for birds and watchers alike. It also boasts Britain's best-known birder's pub, the George at Cley. I must say I tend to keep quiet in there, as ecstasy over the first swallow is not understood by those who converse in the arcane codes of the 300-plus species coterie. The conversation here is spattered with abbreviations like med. gull, wood sand., and BOP. I have even heard of a system by which the identity and whereabouts of a rare species is phoned into the grapevine with maximum speed and economy by the incantation of an eleven-digit number. (Which was most concisely and

effectively parodied by the Bucks Birds Recorder Ron Young-
man who, when I asked him this summer if there were any
local sites where I might hear nightjars, replied that I *might* find
one at 'SU 750894 approx. where in 1976 there was an (un-
mated) ♂. . . . The PH at SU 752899 is very pleasant if you
fail.')

Still, on a visit to north Norfolk early this autumn, Peter
Newmark and myself were sufficiently roused by all this
earnestness to set ourselves the task of seeing a hundred
species in one day. After twelve exhausting hours we had
managed eighty-five. It had been great fun, but also an insight
into the richness and variety of the bird-life along this coast.

Norfolk has long been wise in the ways of managing its
coastal natural resources to preserve their 'power to arouse
emotion'. So it was no great surprise to us that we saw avocets
(the first to nest there for 150 years) from a public hide by the
side of the coast road; that every village was brimming with
swallows and martins; and that the last bird we saw was a dark
and piratical arctic skua, darting about the sea-wall and sailing
dinghies at Blakeney. Its clear message was that, when the tide
comes in, tourists and tickers stop here.

November 1977

It's rutting time again. From Caithness birchwoods and Devon combes mobs of concupiscent does are swarming into the roads, terrorizing motorists and scattering walkers. Monster stags – some all of 4 feet high – are glimpsed posturing among the trees and bellowing with what is, unmistakably, lust. And in one embattled bunker in the Chilterns, strategists from the National Trust, the British Deer Society and the local parish councils sift through the latest crisis reports of vandalized rose-bushes and dented mudguards and decide that this year the annual kill must be raised to 120 does.

Poor deer. They cannot put a hoof right with some people. Their problem, through no fault of their own, is that they are an anachronism, a relic of the medieval countryside which is proving successful enough to get caught up in the cost-benefit equations of modern planning. Our local herd of fallows in Ashridge Park, whose fate (mentioned above) was decided four weeks ago, has been here since the thirteenth century – almost since the Normans introduced this deer to Britain. They started as a monastic herd in about 1270, were hunted by the Black Prince and Henry VIII, and passed eventually into the custody of the Brownlow family. But in 1921 Ashridge had to be sold to meet death duties, and when the National Trust acquired nearly 4000 acres they understandably decided that the old practice of 'emparking' the deer would be both expensive and incompatible with public access to the estate.

That seems to have been the beginning of the trouble. With no natural predators and no restrictions on their movements, the deer have increased both in numbers and in the range of their feeding forays. They munch their way through fields of winter wheat and allotment plots of beans. Frankly, I would give a lot to have them raid my vegetable patch, but many householders (not to mention farmers) do not feel the same, and a feud of considerable bitterness is brewing about their future. The National Trust says that fencing off part of the park would be too costly. The local council begrudges enclosing more than one allotment. Deer lovers greatly outnumber disgruntled horticulturalists, but cannot match their venom; and though one wag has suggested spraying the allotments with lion's urine (from adjacent Whipsnade Zoo) most of the gardeners would prefer the deterrent powers of a machine gun, if one is to judge from their published letters.

And yet the number of animals responsible for all this acrimony is probably not more than 400 (compared to 800 when they were enclosed). There is an annual kill of does, euphemistically called a cull, as if shooting deer was like plucking flowers. There is a bit of poaching. There is, probably capping them both, the slaughter on the roads through the park, which, with the crazily inverted logic of the magistrate who recently called elderly pedestrians a 'danger to motorists', gets the deer branded as a traffic hazard. Most motorists who hit a deer have done so because they ignored the warning signs, and failed to slow down where there are reflective metal plates along the roadsides (to flash headlight beams at potential road-crossers).

One recent hit-and-run casualty was the most magnificent deer in the park, and his life story shows up the dreadful irony of the displacement of these animals. He was a pure white stag, 150 pounds in weight. One night a friend, with once-in-a-lifetime luck, had watched him fighting in the moonlight on his back lawn. Next month he was dead.

It is a sorry situation, with not much compassion in evidence, and no easy solutions. The fact that we are unable to find an economic answer seems to me just one more proof of how sophisticated were the land-use systems of our ancestors. The medieval deer park was an elegant model of multiple land-use, a ranch for growing semi-wild animals and timber, and a recreational area to boot. The deer were kept safe inside, and crops safe outside, by massive stock-proof boundaries – walls, hedges or, more usually, cleft-oak palisades. They must have been enormously expensive to maintain, but by the middle of the fourteenth century there was at least one deer park for every four parishes in England. Some even had complex internal fencing so that deer could coexist with young saplings and arable crops. In Sutton Coldfield Park, which has survived miraculously in the heart of Birmingham, you can still see the pattern of embanked woods ('hursts') surrounding the central grazing plain of grassland and heath.

Many of the more interesting new land-use experiments seem to catch echoes of medieval systems. It's encouraging, for instance, to see the increasing popularity of 'pick-your-own' on farms. A few years ago it was just strawberries. Now the advertising boards go out with the early broad beans and don't come in until the late potatoes. And, seeing whole families out in the fields at weekends, I cannot help thinking how much this new arrangement reflects the best features of the old open field and common system. Everyone benefits. The farmer saves on labour and transport costs. The pickers get cheap, fresh food, a day out in the country, and some intimate contact with growing things. The car doubles-up as tourer and delivery van. The land is being used simultaneously as a farm and a park. The system is proving so successful in the Home Counties that some farmers are having to think about providing landscaped car parks and picnic areas for their visitors. Perhaps, before too long, some enterprising fruit-grower will install some deer in his orchards as well.

In 1976 the television producer John Percival persuaded the BBC to finance a project in which a group of volunteers would live for a year under Iron Age conditions, and be filmed going about their daily business. He outlined the terms of the project exactly in his fine, underrated and honest book:* 'What we set out to do – and this has been much misunderstood – was to see if a group of quite ordinary young people, most of them born and brought up in towns, could learn to live successfully within the limits of an Iron Age technology. It was clearly impossible to recapture the beliefs and superstitions, the skills and experience, the basic social attitudes of prehistoric people, and this was never our intention.'

The fourteen episodes of Living in the Past that came out of the experiment became one of the most obsessively debated series ever put out by the BBC. In general, public response was lukewarm, not to say cynical. Critics found fault with the villagers' youthfulness and middle-class backgrounds (fair comment, though this was what most of the volunteers were), and their lack of manual skills. And though the project's terms of reference were continually restated, viewers took offence whenever the volunteers strayed 'out of period', or took the smallest archaeological liberties. Most of all they objected to the slights cast upon civilization by the volunteers muffing a seemingly crude prehistoric task, or seeming positively to enjoy their state of wretchedness.

I suspect that these ill-tempered reactions said more about the spectators than the participants. As a friend of John Percival, I had been fortunate in being involved with the project from its outset. I'd met the volunteers before they moved in, helped in a small way with their training and with the selection of the site, and eventually had the special privilege of staying at the camp for a few days. Never once did the project seem to me feeble or amateur, and my stay there made me

* *Living in the Past*, BBC Publications, 1980.

170

wish I had volunteered myself. I am grateful that Vole *gave me the opportunity of recapturing what remain the most sensually vivid few days of my life.*

Living in the Past
First published in *Vole*, April 1978

In the aerial shot that opens each episode of *Living in the Past*, the settlement has the look of a raft or an ark, an incarcerated colony adrift in the woods. You can make out the prow and bridge, and the walls, built for a long journey. They are familiar shapes if you walk about the southern chalk hills, where the earthworks of past occupations have much the same look of forlorn hopefulness.

So I was hardly prepared for the thrill of my first glimpse of the camp. I had just turned a corner along a woodland track when the thatched roof of the great hut swam suddenly into view, ringed with wisps of smoke and glinting where new straw caught the winter sunlight. Something that I had only ever seen in drawings or dreamed about, that had been always insubstantial and fanciful, had quite literally come to life, and I had my first real experience of culture shock.

Inside the stockade first impressions came so fast and un-expectedly that I can only remember them in disconnected detail, like a mass of snatched snapshots. Cow's trotters strung up from a pole. A row of wattle and daub beehives. The smell of hides and untreated fleeces hanging in the air like a sharp smoke. People pottering incessantly, even whilst they were talking to you – querning, shelling peas, basket making, spinning. It was only later, when the assault on the senses had quietened a little, that I realized that, whatever it was to the BBC, to the ten volunteers this makeshift ancient monument was *home*.

A second visit, on a bright, early spring day. There are other guests about. One, an anthropologist, is showing the volunteers different aboriginal techniques for creating fire, a skill they have so far failed to master. Once they know the tricks (it helps to have two pairs of hands, working in relay, to keep up the speed of the drilling rod) they have a fire going in half an hour. It goes down on film, and the villagers go back to their own concerns. They have kept their own fire going continuously for twelve months and at this stage they are more interested in what the prehistorian being filmed on the other side of the camp is saying about them. He believes the experiment to be archaeologically devalued because the community did not adopt a hierarchical structure. The volunteers are resentful that he will not argue out this point with them on film. They believe that they could never have coped temperamentally with such a structure. Neither they nor producer John Percival have ever seen the project as an exercise in impersonation or method-acting. You cannot shed twentieth-century consciousness just be wearing animal skins for a year. What is important is the interplay between the two cultures, the new perspectives that emerge when modern people are obliged to use a primitive technology. All of them see the project as an *exploration* of another culture rather than a copy.

The visitors leave and the farm gets back to business. The goats have to be milked, work on the cart resumed and Sarah's birthday celebrated. The preoccupations of people living on their own wits and resources have not changed much in 2,000 years. They must survive, create wealth against the bad times, and enjoy themselves when they can.

It is the ineluctable power of darkness that strikes you most sharply when you come here from a culture dependent on electricity. The pattern of life is governed absolutely by the hours of daylight. You move indoors with the dusk, get up with the dawn. In the long winter nights the team often used to stay in bed for fourteen hours. Inside the hut itself, with its two low entrances, it is permanently twilight. The central fire lights up a circle a few yards wide, but it takes minutes for your eyes to adjust and take in the complex architecture in the far recesses.

The hut is over 50 feet wide and everything from store-chambers to bread ovens has been crammed in. The layout has a logic, when you can see it plainly. The looms are near the doorway so that the weavers can work in the dry but also in natural light. The odd-shaped cuts of meat, strung about the roof like macabre Christmas decorations, are there to catch the smoke. The little wattled cubicles – one for each couple – that lie against the perimeter walls also make sense, though true Ancient Brits may have been less concerned about privacy. The volunteers all missed this greatly, and as the communal hut took three months longer to complete than they had expected, they were grateful for the small oases of quiet their cells eventually provided.

Yet the fire draws them together. It has burned out a lot of tensions in the group, and forges a peculiar kind of temporary intimacy. It is remarkable how living in a circular space with the light source in the centre can shape your relationships with your cohabitants. You face in, towards each other. It is always the nearsides of things and people that are lit up. It is surprising, too, what you can do in a circle round a fire if you have to. You can have a bath, mend a shoe, even eat a soft-boiled egg without a plate – if you have practised enough. And that scene, I suppose, sums up the image which many critics have of the experiment. It is a banal party game: holding the ring; charades; a kind of musical chairs in which it is not you that revolves precariously around, but the world – a cup, a loaf, an argument, a whole reconstructed version of history. And so it can seem, until it is your forfeit. Clumsy at the best of times, and hopeless in the dark, I spilt the drink and dropped my egg. Worst of all I upset the salt, which is a scarce product they have to trade for, and as I shamefacedly tried to shovel it back from the earth floor, I had a sharp lesson in value scales.

Using the BBC as a middleman the members of the team have incorporated trade with the outside world into their economic system. They bartered the surplus of young animals they had in the summer for salt and extra honey. When they heard about the bread strike in the winter, they went into mass production of their loaves – stoneground to a fault – and got venison in return from the locals. With more common sense than some of their critics, they have seen that these occasional indulgences in twentieth-century foods do not compromise the spirit of the project one jot. So, with bed and board to trade for, and a birthday to celebrate, I had taken in a good supply of alcohol to add to their own potently sharp mead, and we stayed up very late.

Helped by the community of the fire, they talked about their year. They still remember the early months with bitterness, the bad advice they had been given, the claustrophobic rain, most of all the back-breaking hay harvest. It had taken them six weeks on their knees, working with small hand sickles, to cut the 3 acres of grass and carry it back half a mile to camp. There was a good deal of disillusionment at this time. No one objected to hard work, but was that really all there was? In Programme 3, Sharon – hair tied neatly back in a way that said a good deal about her disenchantment with barbarianism – spoke for them all. They had hoped to be 'Iron Agers' and had turned into builders' labourers. Any lingering fantasies that donning a hand-woven shift would be like taking a trip – the gateway to an instant expansion of historical conscious-ness – were rapidly lost. But was it too much to hope that they might have time to use their imaginations a little? If they could not, the experiment would indeed be nothing more than a meaningless re-enactment, a kind of historical mime.

I realize now that I was not wholly immune from the 'changed consciousness' fallacy myself. I think I had expected (and half hoped for) a more complete rout of modernism – a surrender to mysticism or primeval terrors, perhaps, or the evolution of a private language, at least something *different* about them. Well, there was. They were surer, sharper, more relaxed than when I had met them before the experiment. Whatever illusions they had had about the experiment had dissolved, and they were beginning to enjoy the challenge of making a going concern of a pre-industrial technology. The chat round the fire that night was more like that in a senior common room than a charged encounter group. They talked about the habits of owls, the merits of pair-bonding, and the more arcane reaches of prehistoric scholarship. I was struck especially by how openly they would talk amongst themselves about others in the group who could hear what they were saying.

The temptation to opt out had stayed with each one of them since those first hard months, and on this particular evening they were still concerned with the last successfully suppressed 'escape'. (There had been a few temporary disappearances that the press, thankfully, had not found out about.) John, a keen bird-watcher, had been visited by friends with news of a rare bird (a wallcreeper) wintering in Cheddar Gorge. It was a once-in-a-lifetime chance and only a short car journey away. There were long heart-searching talks. No one wanted John to go, and though it was a last-minute decision, he stayed at home. In the end they are quite clear about their loyalties to each other, and about what constitutes 'cheating'. An indulgent day out in a car is very different from a celebratory bowl of light ale.

The counterpart of the frankness that has resulted from living and working in close contact is the very great care they take of each other. They were trying, this evening, to work out a way of recompensing John for his disappointment, and were thinking about all taking him to see the wallcreeper on the day the farm closed down.

My own contribution was about as accomplished as my handling of the salt, and I realized how far they had progressed in the art of speaking one's mind without rancour. I was offered a spare cell for the night, but did not think I could face my confusions in the pitch black, and curled up by the fire for company, wrapped up in a sheepskin.

A short while later there was a curious episode that confirmed their cohesion as a group, and exposed still more of my preconceptions. I couldn't sleep in these unfamiliar surroundings and at about one in the morning noticed that the villagers were coming out of their cells, talking earnestly by the fire and going out of the hut in relays. For a moment, I must confess, I presumed this to be the signs of the sexual liberality I'd also expected. But when I got up to investigate I found that Brian hadn't 'come in yet'. Inspired by the mead, no doubt, he'd wandered off to gaze at the stars, and with touching maternal concern the villagers were worried in case he'd fallen down a ditch or tripped over an animal, and were scouring the site for him. He turned up eventually, and everyone settled back to their private attachments.

Morning starts slowly, but decisively. Everyone knows their job and when to begin it. The pair who are responsible for the food that day are up first, have the fire stoked, and breakfast – a standard dish of boiled wheat, honey and goat's milk, not far removed from frumenty – simmering in the cauldron before anyone else is awake. Today the cooks are Martin and Helen. For the rest of the day they will have complete responsibility for gathering firewood, butchering meat, preparing vegetables, and providing three meals for the community. But the responsibilities of the cooking-pair are more complex than the simple provision of food. In a sense they are stewards for the day. They must keep the fire going and manage one of the community's most precious resources – continuously boiling water. There is only one large iron pot in which water can be boiled for any period (their clay pots tend to break up) and anything less important than cooking – and this includes washing-up, bathing and dying wool – normally has to make do with momentarily hot water, produced by plunging red-hot lumps of iron into bowls.

After breakfast everyone gets on with their chosen (or allotted) task with the minimum of fuss. Jill and Sharon go out to plough with the two Dexter cows and a single-bladed wooden share. They finish sixty furrows that morning. Martin begins to butcher the rabbits they caught yesterday, Helen to make dumplings out of flour and pig lard. I go out with Kate, Sarah and the two Johns to forage. I am thinking the first wild vegetables may be showing their shoots and take a basket, but they bring Sirius, the farm's sparky little lurcher, whose reputation as a hunter-gatherer does not rest on her botanical skills. She tears off through the woods at regular intervals after invisible quarry. I am uneasy and the girls are delighted. They have overcome their qualms about hunting and now positively relish it. They know what Sirius is chasing by the calls she makes.

In the end we go back with a basket of hedge garlic for the rabbit stew and an exhausted but unfulfilled dog. It is a curious scene at the camp, the women returning from the fields and the hunt, the men working in the kitchen and the yard. The blurring of sexual roles (which owes as much to twentieth-century liberalism as Celtic sociology) runs right through the pattern of life on the farm. Everyone, regardless of sex, has done their share of the hard graft of building, ploughing and reaping. Everyone querns three bowls of flour a day. It is only in their relationships with animals that any significant division seems to have evolved: the men kill the bigger animals and the women milk them. How much this is due to purely physical factors – the men also do the other heavy axe work, for instance – and how much to the symbolic meaning of these acts, is difficult to tell.

Apart from the extraordinary achievement of living success-fully together, most of the villagers regard their relationships with animals as the experience which has affected them most deeply. It is not hard to appreciate this. Nowhere in the farm are you removed from close physical contact with animals, in varying stages of life and death. Goats roam about outside the stockade, and chickens and polecats inside. You wake up to the undeniable summons of a cockerel *inside* the hut, go to bed in skins that are still sticky with lanolin. You cannot sit down for long without a dog or calf touching you, or avert your gaze from the hard visual evidence of slaughter. Flayed heads and hides hang from the trees, entirely functionally, but grim totems to a novitiate like myself who has not been through the rites of killing.

This constant intimacy has helped them through the painful conflicts of killing animals they had come to know and love. Like others before them they have found, paradoxically, that it is easier to kill, for food, an animal you have held and nourished yourself. Except for the vegetarian Ainsworths (who left the experiment before Christmas) they have become progressively more enthusiastic carnivores, encouraged no doubt by a surfeit of Celtic beans. The men became such adept butchers that they once killed and decapitated a ram for the cameras before the focus could be changed. That they then went into a slapstick routine of trying to stick the head back on for a re-take is typical of the odd mixture of affection and matter-of-factness they show towards their animals. They joke a good deal about killing – especially Martin, who, as the village's qualified doctor, is well aware of the role of operating-theatre humour. They would not hurt a hair of the mice that live in the goat-hut; they even have pet names for them. But when rats invaded their grain store and haystacks – the harvest they had nearly broken their backs getting in – they went for them in a bloodcurdling orgy of vengeance. They killed the lot, babies included, and ate the biggest in a stew.

It is an afternoon in early March. There are only three weeks to go. Most of the housework has been done and the villagers are about their private schemes. Kate and Sarah are lounging against the haystack playing with the polecats and spinning desultorily. Pete, John and Brian are working on the cart, their biggest piece of wooden technology yet. Brian is turning pegs on a pole lathe and Pete is shaping a solid 3-foot-diameter wheel with axe blows of deadly accuracy. Shaggy Maggie, a nanny goat with ineffably gentle manners and a passion for carpentry, nibbles away the rough edges. It is an idyll a pre-Raphaelite would have been proud of. Their skills and sense of ease are unrecognizable when compared with the awkward fumbling of their early months. Although their admiration of real Iron Agers increases with each new experiment, they have created a perfectly viable economy of their own. They are producing new resources faster than they are using them up. They understand the annual cycle of work better now, and that the months of numbing summer labour are rewarded with months of leisure. That is what they are enjoying enormously now, and what has seemed the ultimate effrontery to some viewers.

The moments they will remember most have almost all been embellishments above the call of duty, as they probably are with all cultures: the clay hair-washes, the contoured wood loo seat; the 20-foot-tall wicker man they burned for the festival of Samhain; the lyre strung with stretched sheepgut; the fat trouser legs woven on tubular looms; the day they went tobogganing with the pigs whilst the rest of the West Country was paralysed under snow (they helped with car rescue, too); and another, warmer day when, desperate for wind, they climbed the hill and winnowed on the crest of the downs, a vision for the passers-by; and their 'trifles' – vast follies of cake and mead and fruit they cook on birthdays to make up for their yearning for sweets.

It's true that they might not have been so relaxed if they had had to prepare for another year; that they have not had the economic drain of child rearing. Yet the skill with which they can now work as a secondary activity suggests that they would have coped very well with a growing population.

All of which proves nothing. Iron Age culture was obviously viable, otherwise we wouldn't be here now. The strength of *Living in the Past* seems to me that it happened in the *present*, that it was a celebration of perennial hardiness as much as a proof of ancient skills. Whether the experiment was archeologically authentic is largely academic. It was a compromise from the outset, set up to provide material for a television series, and should be judged as a story, not as history. As such it seems to me to have a touch of the stuff out of which myths are made. Not the story of 'Iron Age Man', particularly; certainly not the myth of 'Noble Savage' (the villagers are neither). It is closer to the ageless story of the peasant, who for some thousands of years lived (and still live in many parts of the world) lives of ingenuity, endurance and independence without ripping the planet to bits. *Living in the Past* is a reworking – a reliving, you might say – of this story through modern imaginations. To me its greatest contribution is yet another counter to the belief, desperately clung to by highly industrial civilizations, that life under earlier technologies was inexorably nasty, brutish, short and joyless.

In a few weeks the camp will be demolished and the villagers will pick up the threads of their previous lives. Since it is the business of myths to provide inspiration, I rather hope they think of a name for the settlement before then, for it would be good for us to be able to go on telling stories about them – the group of young people in Wessex who worked out their own version of a very old parable about man and the earth.

PART SIX

'Far other worlds'

The Promised Landscape

First published in the series 'My Fantasy World' in
Good Housekeeping, June 1981

It's hard to have original fantasies these days. The dreamtime is fuelled by great communal longings, and is full of converging Arcadian visions – green, pleasant, pacific and handwoven. You may regret these collectivist tendencies or rejoice in them, but there's no getting away from the fact: Eden is commonland.

My favourite Utopia was set down as long ago as the fourteenth century by the writer of that wonderful alliterative poem, *Piers Plowman*. William Langland fell asleep on a hilltop in the Malverns ('In a somer season whan soft was the sonne' – he was fantasizing before he began) and had a vision of the whole kingdom of England as

A faire feld ful of folke. . . .
Of alle manner of men, the mene and the riche
Worchyng and wandryng as the world asketh

A modern, Alternative Service-style version has rendered down this last line as 'moving busily about their worldly affairs', which is hardly the stuff that dreams are made of. But looking back, as one often does when imagining forward, I can remember a time when the countryside was indeed full of people, worchyng and wandryng, and am happy to report that these activities had nothing whatever to do with mundane industriousness.

It's become fashionable to lament the overcrowding of the countryside, as if the fields were at this very moment being choked by some kind of human pollutant. But this is not the impression you get if you stray just a little way from the roads. Here you will see not an overpopulated landscape, but one being drained of figures just as surely as it is losing its colour and variety.

When I was a child, twenty-five years ago, I can remember the woods and fields brimming with other children, climbing trees, building camps, cooking, trading, tramping about the footpaths in little packs reciting rude limericks, and disappearing into the bushes for private experiments. The older ones would sometimes wander off in pairs, and we would catch enthralling, ethereal glimpses of them in pink tangles under the hedges, or glowing palely under the moon in harvest fields. Now the only loving couples you see are wedged into the back seats of parked cars.

I enjoy solitude as much as anyone, but I do not relish barrenness, and I view fields fleeced of folk as unnatural, unjust and full of foreboding. I have a persistent vision of them reclaimed by people up to all possible versions, authorized or not, of worchyng and wandryng.

I hope no one misunderstands this. I don't wish any blight upon our farmers and landowners. But I don't think I am alone in hoping that they might soon begin to take their social obligations as seriously as their economic, and play the role of stewards that, as they frequently tell us, is theirs by dint of profession. I wish them continued good fortune in escaping the axe applied to every other sphere of public subsidy, but I confess that I do still dream of the day when there is more reciprocity in our relationships, and farmers say a small thank you to the taxpayers for keeping them in business (and free of planning controls) by allowing them to enjoy their investments a little more. . . .

The day is Rogation Sunday to be precise, the traditional date for the beating of the bounds, and the day appointed for the annual celebration of the new access rights. The processions follow the routes not just of the parish boundaries before local-government reorganisation, but of all ancient footpaths and tracks. Here and there the assembly halts for a small bonfire, on which is thrown any illegal fencing and the odd 'Private' notice which has not found its way into a rural museum. These bonfires apparently commemorate the martyr-dom of St Ubble, who was burned to death in one of the great conflagrations of the old farming order, somewhere near the sacrificial site known as M4. (These ceremonial fires occasionally used to be encouraged to spread to plantations of Scandianavian conifers. But there aren't many of these left now, and the practice has been discouraged out of courtesy to the Swedes who are, by custom, honoured guests on each parish procession. Sweden has always had a Right of Common Access – *allemansraat* – over virtually its whole land surface, and Swedish advisers were present on all the early processions. The custom stuck.)

But it is at harvest time that the differences between the old farming landscape and the new are most conspicuous. The arable prairies of East Anglia, for instance, are now the most extraordinary chequerboards of colour, a mosaic of vegetable patches in every stage of leaf, flower and fruit. The change happened quite quickly. Landowners, faced with prohibitive prices for fuel and fertilizer, realized that the most logical and economical extension of 'Pay-and-pick' crops was 'Pay-and-grow', and began leasing out their land in strips along lines that were scarcely distinguishable from the medieval open field system. The most eager tenants were health-food enthusiasts from north London and the Stour Valley, many of whom gave up the dole to tend their vast new allotments. As a result, the vegetable fields of central Norfolk, garlanded with the flowers of Jerusalem artichokes, asparagus-peas and pumpkins, have become as great a tourist attraction in blossom time as the fruit orchards of Kent.

In those areas where cereal crops are still raised intensively the ancient practice of gleaning has been revived, and many families find they are able to gather enough grain for their Moulinex blenders to keep them in wholemeal flour for the winter.

Orchards are as busy and beautiful as they were before the days of Golden Delicious, but are enormously increased in number now that every parish has its own communal fruit garden. Even towns and cities have municipal orchards, since planners realized that their traditional objection to planting fruiting as well as flowering cherries – 'But the public may *pick* them' – was ludicrous. The widespread enthusiasm for farming has also resulted in some fascinating experiments in vertical cropping, and vines can be seen trained hundreds of feet above pavement level on the walls of office blocks.

Now that the countryside is more accessible (and the people, incidentally, much healthier) the British winter is no longer something to be reviled and hidden from. There has been a resurgence of informal winter sports and frolics and some ingenious new inventions. Now there's no need to produce butter mountains to satisfy the whims of EEC economists, the hills have been given over for public enjoyment, and mud-tobogganing has become a national craze.

In London the chic event of winter is no longer the New Beaujolais race but what has become known as 'First Faggot'. The ancient trees in Epping Forest are lopped for firewood every winter, just as they were in the nineteenth century (the forest is so light and airy as a result that primroses have returned to bloom), and on the first day of the cutting season, teams race to cut and cart the first bundle to the wood-burning stove in El Vino's.

Meanwhile, in front of wood fires all round the country, parents tell their children tales about the time when the land and the things that grew on it were regarded as exclusively private property. The children treat it as a wonderful tall story, and have invented an energetic new game called 'Farmers, keepers'.